1984

CONVERSATIONS
WITH IGOR STRAVINSKY

CONVERSATIONS
WITH
IGOR STRAVINSKY

IGOR STRAVINSKY

and

ROBERT CRAFT

University of California Press

Berkeley and Los Angeles

University of California Press
Berkeley and Los Angeles

© 1958, 1959 by Igor Stravinsky

First California Paperback Printing 1980
ISBN 0-520-04040-6
All Rights Reserved

Printed in the United States of America

2 3 4 5 6 7 8 9

*Library of Congress Cataloging in
Publication Data*

Stravinskiĭ, Igor′ Fedorovich, 1882-1971.
  Conversations with Igor Stravinsky.

  Includes index
  1. Music. 2. Stravinskiĭ. Igor′ Fedorovich,
1882-1971. I. Craft, Robert. II. Title.
ML410.S932A33   1980   780   79-19367

In the Kingdom of the Father there is no drama but only dialogue, which is disguised monologue.

—Rudolph Kassner

ACKNOWLEDGEMENTS

Acknowledgements and thanks are due to Madame de Tinan for permission to reprint letters by Claude Debussy; to Madame Jacques Rivière for letters by Jacques Rivière; to Monsieur Edouard Ravel for letters by Maurice Ravel; and to the Trustees for the copyrights of the late Dylan Thomas for letters by Dylan Thomas.

CONTENTS

Contents

ILLUSTRATIONS

13

Illustrations

1

ABOUT COMPOSING AND COMPOSITIONS

R.C. When did you become aware of your vocation as a composer?

I.S. I do not remember when and how I first thought of myself as a composer. All I remember is that these thoughts started very early in my childhood, long before any serious musical study.

R.C. The musical idea: when do you recognize it as an idea?

I.S. When something in my nature is satisfied by some aspect of an auditive shape. But long before ideas are born I begin work by relating intervals rhythmically. This exploration of possibilities is always conducted at the piano. Only after I have established my melodic or harmonic relationships do I pass to composition. Composition is a later expansion and organization of material.

R.C. Is it always clear in your mind from the inception of the idea what form of composition will develop? And the idea itself: is it clear what instrumental sound will produce it?

I.S. You should not suppose that once the musical idea is in your mind you will see more or less distinctly the form your composition may evolve. Nor will the sound (timbre) always be present. But if the musical idea is merely a group of notes, a motive coming suddenly to your mind, it very often comes together with its sound.

R.C. You say that you are a doer, not a thinker; that composing is not a department of conceptual thinking; that your nature is to compose music and you compose it naturally, not by acts of thought or will. A few hours of work on about one-third of the days of the last fifty years have produced a catalogue which testifies that composing is indeed natural to you. But how is nature approached?

I.S. When my main theme has been decided I know on general lines what kind of musical material it will require. I start to look for this material, sometimes playing old masters (to put myself in motion), sometimes starting directly to improvise rhythmic units on a provisional row of notes (which can become a final row). I thus form my building material.

R.C. When you achieve the music you have been working to create, are you always sure of it, do you always instantly recognize it as finished, or do you sometimes have to try it for a greater period of time?

I.S. Usually I recognize my find. But when I am unsure of it I feel uncomfortable in postponing a solution and in relying on the future. The future never gives me the assurance of reality I receive from the present.

R.C. What is theory in musical composition?

I.S. Hindsight. It doesn't exist. There are compositions from which it is deduced. Or, if this isn't quite true, it has a by-product existence that is powerless to create or even to justify. Nevertheless, composition involves a deep intuition of theory.

R.C. Do musical ideas occur to you at random times of the day or night?

I.S. Ideas usually occur to me while I am composing, and only very rarely do they present themselves when I am away from my work. I am always disturbed if they come to my ear when

1. Stravinsky with his parents, Hamburg-vor-der-Höhe, 1895

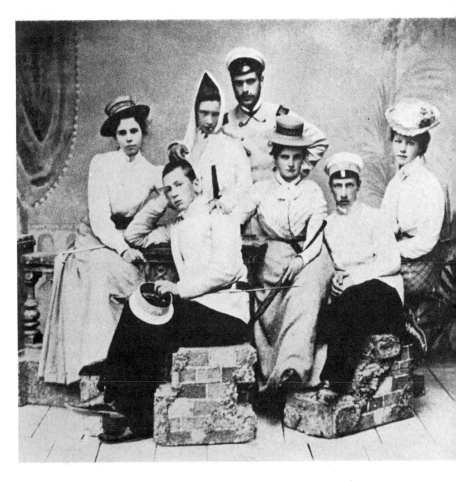

2. Near Oustiloug (Volynski Government), 1900

Stravinsky (wearing cap, beardless) with his brothers Goury (1884-1917, ho
ing cap in hand), Youry (1879-1941, whose two daughters are still livi
in Leningrad), and his Nossenko cousins, Catherine Nossenko (in hood, w
became Stravinsky's wife in 1906), Ludmilla (extreme right), her sister, and V
Nossenko (extreme left, a cousin of Catherine's, and an M.D. still living
Switzerland). The remaining woman is another Nossenko, Vera's sister

my pencil is missing and I am obliged to keep them in my memory by repeating to myself their intervals and rhythm. It is very important to me to remember the pitch of the music at its first appearance: if I transpose it for some reason I am in danger of losing the freshness of first contact and I will have difficulty in recapturing its attractiveness. Music has sometimes appeared to me in dreams, but only on one occasion have I been able to write it down. This was during the composition of *L'Histoire du Soldat*, and I was surprised and happy with the result. Not only did the music appear to me but the person performing it was present in the dream as well. A young gypsy was sitting by the edge of the road. She had a child on her lap for whose entertainment she was playing a violin. The motive she kept repeating used the whole bow, or, as we say in French, 'avec toute la longueur de l'archet'. The child was very enthusiastic about the music and applauded it with his little hands. I, too, was very pleased with it, was especially pleased to be able to remember it, and I joyfully included this motive in the music of the *Petit Concert*.

R.C. You often speak of the weight of an interval. What do you mean?

I.S. I lack words and have no gift for this sort of thing anyway, but perhaps it will help if I say that when I compose an interval I am aware of it as an object (when I think about it in that way at all, that is), as something outside me, the contrary of an impression.

Let me tell you about a dream that came to me while I was composing *Threni*. After working late one night I retired to bed still troubled by an interval. I dreamed about this interval. It had become an elastic substance stretching exactly between the two notes I had composed, but underneath these notes at either end was an egg, a large testicular egg. The eggs were gelatinous to the touch (I touched them), and warm, and they were protected by nests. I woke up knowing that my interval was right. (For those who want more of the dream, it was pink—I often dream in colour. Also, I was so surprised to see the eggs I immediately understood them to be symbols. Still in the dream I went to my library of dictionaries and looked up 'interval', but found only a confusing explanation which I checked the next morning in reality and found to be the same.)

R.C. While composing do you ever think of any audience? Is there such a thing as a problem of communication?

I.S. When I compose something, I cannot conceive that it should fail to be recognized for what it is, and understood. I use the language of music, and my statement in my grammar will be clear to the musician who has followed music up to where my contemporaries and I have brought it.

R.C. Have you ever thought that music is as Auden says 'a virtual image of our experience of living as temporal, with its double aspect of recurrence and becoming'?

I.S. If music is to me an 'image of our experience of living as temporal' (and however unverifiable, I suppose it is), my saying so is the result of a reflection, and as such is independent of music itself. But this kind of thinking about music is a different vocation altogether for me: I cannot *do* anything with it as a truth, and my mind is a *doing* one. Auden means 'Western' music or, as he would say, 'music as history'; jazz improvisation is the dissipation of the time image and, if I understand 'recurrence' and 'becoming', their aspect is greatly diminished in serial music. Auden's 'image of our experience of living as temporal' (which is also an image) is above music, perhaps, but it does not obstruct or contradict the purely

18

musical experience. What shocks me, however, is the discovery that many people think below music. Music is merely something that reminds them of something else—of landscapes, for example; my *Apollo* is always reminding someone of Greece. But in even the most specific attempts at evocation, what is meant by being 'like', and what are 'correspondences'? Who, listening to Liszt's precise and perfect little *Nuages gris*, could pretend that 'grey clouds' are a musical cause and effect?

R.C. Do you work with a dialectical conception of form? Is the word meaningful in musical terms?

I.S. Yes to both questions, in so far as the art of dialectics is, according to the dictionaries, the art of logical discussion. Musical form is the result of the 'logical discussion' of musical materials.

R.C. I have often heard you say 'an artist must avoid symmetry but he may construct in parallelisms'. What do you mean?

I.S. The mosaics at Torcello of the Last Judgment are a good example. Their subject is division, division, moreover, into two halves suggesting equal halves. But, in fact, each is the other's complement, not its equal nor its mirror, and the dividing line itself is not a perfect perpendicular. On the one side skulls with, in the sockets, lightning-shaped snakes, and on the other, Eternal Life (those white figures, I wonder if Tintoretto didn't know them), are balanced, but not equally balanced. And, the sizes and proportions, movements and rests, darks and lights of the two sides are always varied.

Mondrian's *Blue Façade* (*composition 9, 1914*) is a nearer example of what I mean. It is composed of elements that tend to symmetry but in fact avoids symmetry in subtle parallelisms. Whether or not the suggestion of symmetry is avoidable in the art of architecture, whether it is natural to architecture, I do not know. However, painters who paint architectural subject matter and borrow architectural designs are often guilty of it. And only the master musicians have managed to avoid it in periods whose architecture has embodied aesthetic idealisms, i.e., when architecture was symmetry and symmetry was confused with form itself. Of all the musicians of his age Haydn was the most aware, I think, that to be perfectly symmetrical is to be perfectly dead. We are some of us still divided by an illusory compulsion towards 'classical' symmetry on the one hand, and by the desire to compose as purely non-symmetrically as the Incas, on the other.

R.C. Do you regard musical form as in some degree mathematical?

I.S. It is at any rate far closer to mathematics than to literature—not perhaps to mathematics itself, but certainly to something like mathematical thinking and mathematical relationships. (How misleading are all literary descriptions of musical form!) I am not saying that composers think in equations or charts of numbers, nor are those things more able to symbolize music. But the way composers think, the way I think, is, it seems to me, not very different from mathematical thinking. I was aware of the similarity of these two modes while I was still a student; and, incidentally, mathematics was the subject that most interested me in school. Musical form is mathematical because it is ideal, and form is always ideal, whether it is, as Ortega y Gasset wrote 'an image of memory or a construction of ours'. But though it may be mathematical, the composer must not seek mathematical formulae.

R.C. You often say that to compose is to solve a problem. Is it no more than that?

I.S. Seurat said: 'Certain critics have done me the honour to see poetry in what I do, but I paint by my method with no other thought in mind.'

R.C. In your Greek-subject pieces *Apollo, Oedipus, Orpheus, Persephone*, dotted rhythms are of great importance (the opening of *Apollo*; the canonic interlude in *Orpheus*; the

'Underworld' music in *Persephone*; the *Oedipus* 'Nonne Monstrum' aria). Is the use of these rhythms conscious stylistic reference to the eighteenth century?

I.S.   Dotted rhythms are characteristic eighteenth-century rhythms. My uses of them in these and other works of that period, such as the introduction to my piano Concerto, are conscious stylistic references. I attempted to build a new music on eighteenth-century classicism using the constructive principles of that classicism (which I cannot define here) and even evoking it stylistically by such means as dotted rhythms.

R.C.   Valéry said: 'We can construct in orderly fashion only by means of conventions.' How do we recognize those conventions in, say, Webern's songs with clarinet and guitar?

I.S.   We don't. An entirely new principle of order is found in the Webern songs which in time will be recognized and conventionalized. But Valéry's essentially classical *dicta* do not foresee that new conventions can be created.

R.C.   A novelist (Isherwood) once complained to you of his difficulties in a technical question of narration. You advised him to find a model. How do you model in music?

I.S.   As I have just described in the case of eighteenth-century dotted rhythms; I have modelled this conventional rhythmic device so that I could 'construct in orderly fashion'.

R.C.   Why did you dispense with bar lines in the *Diphonas* and *Elegias* of the *Threni*?

I.S.   The voices are not always in rhythmic unison. Therefore, any bar lines would cut at least one line arbitrarily. There are no strong beats in these canons, in any case, and the conductor must merely count the music out as he counts out a motet by Josquin. For the same reasons I have also written half notes rather than tied notes over bars. This is perhaps more difficult to read, but it is a truer notation.

R.C.   Did you model your *Threni* on the *Lamentations* of any old master, as, for example, you modelled some dances for *Agon* from de Lauze's *Apologie de la Danse* and from Mersenne's musical examples?

I.S. I had studied Palestrina's complete service, and the *Lamentations* of Tallis and Byrd but I don't think there is any 'influence' of these masters in my music.

R.C. Why do contemporary composers tend to use smaller note values for the beat than did nineteenth-century composers, quaver beats instead of crotchet, and semiquavers instead of quavers? Your music contains many examples of this tendency (the second movement of the *Symphony in C* which is in quaver and semiquaver beats, and the final piece of the *Duo Concertant* which is in semiquaver beats). If you were to double the note values of this music, rewrite it in crotchets and quavers, how would it affect the music in your mind? Also, do you always think or see the note unit as you compose, and have you ever rewritten anything in different note values after it was composed? Your 1943 revision of the *Danse Sacrale* from the *Sacre du Printemps* doubles the values from semiquavers to quavers; was this done to facilitate reading (does it facilitate reading)? Do you believe the size of the note has a relation to the character of the music?

I.S. I don't think you are entirely correct in assuming an evolution from minim to crotchet to quaver pulsations. Contemporary music has created a much greater range and variety of tempi and a vastly greater rhythmic range, therefore the greater range and variety of rhythmic unit (see any table of notation and compare the types of rhythmic unit in use in the last five centuries with those in use today). We write fast tempo music or slow tempo music in large or small note values depending on the music. That is my only explanation.

As a composer I associate a certain kind of music, a certain tempo of music, with a certain kind of note unit. I compose directly that way. There is no act of selection or translation, and the unit of the note and the tempo appear in my imagination at the same time as the interval itself. Only rarely, too, have I found that my original beat unit has led me into notation difficulties. The *Dithyrambe* in the *Duo Concertant*, however, is one such example.

It is difficult for me to judge whether a work of mine translated into larger or smaller note units but played in the same tempo would make an aural difference to me. However, I know that I could not look at the music in its translated state, for the shape of the notes as one writes them is the shape of the original conception itself. (Of course the performer with his different approach will regard the whole problem of notation as a matter of choice, but this is wrong.)

I *do* believe in a relation between the *character* of my music and the kind of note unit of the pulsation, and I do not care that this may be undemonstrable—it is demonstrable to me on the composer's side simply because I think that way. And, conventions have not worked universally for so long that we may deny that there is any relation of ear and eye. Who can take from dictation a passage of contemporary music in 6/4 and tell whether in fact it is not 6/8 or 6/16?

The point of legibility. I did translate my *Danse Sacrale* into larger note values to facilitate reading (of course it is more readable, the reduction in rehearsal time proves that).[1] But legibility and larger note values go together only up to a point. This idea of fast music in white notes applies only to certain types of music (the first movement of my *Symphony in C*, for example, and the *Gloria Patri* in Monteverdi's *Laudate Pueri* from the *Vespers*) but this question cannot be dissociated from the question of bar units and of the rhythmic construction of the music itself.

---

[1] I was also obliged to recopy the first movement of my *Ebony Concerto* in quavers, when the 'jazz' musicians, for whom it was written, proved themselves unable to read semiquavers.

Perhaps the present lack of universal conventions may be interpreted as a blessing; the performer can only profit from a situation in which he is obliged to review his prejudices and develop reading versatility.

R.C. Metres. Can the same effect be achieved by means of accents as by varying the metres? What are bar lines?

I.S. To the first question my answer is, up to a point, yes, but that point is the degree of real regularity in the music. The bar line is much much more than a mere accent and I don't believe that it can be simulated by an accent, at least not in my music.

R.C. In your own music, identity is established by melodic, rhythmic, and other means, but especially by tonality. Do you think you will ever abandon the tonal identification?

I.S. Possibly. We can still create a sense of return to exactly the same place without tonality: musical rhyme can accomplish the same thing as poetic rhyme. But form cannot exist without identity of some sort.

R.C. What is your feeling now about the use of music as accompaniment to recitation (*Persephone*)?

I.S. Do not ask. Sins cannot be undone, only forgiven.

THE SERIES

R.C. Do you think of the intervals in your series as tonal intervals; that is, do your intervals always exert tonal pull?

I.S. The intervals of my series are attracted by tonality; I compose vertically and that is, in one sense at least, to compose tonally.

R.C. How has composing with a series affected your own harmonic thinking? Do you work in the same way—that is, hear relationships and then compose them?

I.S. I hear certain possibilities and I choose. I can create my choice

24

in serial composition just as I can in any tonal contrapuntal form. I hear harmonically, of course, and I compose in the same way I always have.

R.C. Nevertheless, the Gigue from your *Septet* and the choral canons in the *Canticum Sacrum* are much more difficult to hear harmonically than any earlier music of yours. Hasn't composing with a series therefore affected your harmonic scope?

I.S. It is certainly more difficult to hear harmonically the music you speak of than my earlier music; but any serial music intended to be heard vertically is more difficult to hear. The rules and restrictions of serial writing differ little from the rigidity of the great contrapuntal schools of old. At the same time they widen and enrich harmonic scope; one starts to hear more things and differently than before. The serial technique I use impels me to greater discipline than ever before.

R.C. Do you think your time world is the same for the kind of music you are now composing and for your music of thirty-five years ago (*Mavra*, piano Sonata, piano Concerto, *Apollo*)?

I.S. My past and present time worlds cannot be the same. I know that portions of *Agon* contain three times as much music for the same clock length as some other pieces of mine. Naturally, a new demand for greater in-depth listening changes time perspective. Perhaps also the operation of memory in a non-tonally developed work (tonal, but not eighteenth-century tonal system) is different. We are located in time constantly in a tonal-system work, but we may only 'go through' a polyphonic work, whether Josquin's *Duke Hercules Mass* or a serially composed non-tonal-system work.

R.C. Do you find any similarity in the time worlds of oriental music and of certain recent examples of serial music?

I.S. I do not think anything in the nature of the serial idea makes series in essence 'oriental'. Schoenberg himself was a cabalist, of course, but that is merely a personal preoccupation. We

25

have all remarked a monotony (not in any pejorative sense) that we call 'oriental' in serial works, in Boulez's *Le marteau sans maître* for instance. But the kind of monotony we have in mind is characteristic of many kinds of polyphonic music. Our notion of what is oriental is an association of instrumentation chiefly, but also of rhythmic and melodic designs—a very superficial kind of association indeed. I myself have no habit of anything oriental, and especially no measure of time in oriental music. In fact, my attitude resembles that of Henri Micheaux: in the Orient I recognize myself as a barbarian— that excellent word invented by Attic Greeks to designate a people who could not answer them in Attic Greek.

TECHNIQUE

R.C. What is technique?

I.S. The whole man. We learn how to use it but we cannot acquire it in the first place; or, perhaps I should say that we are born with the ability to acquire it. At present it has come to mean the opposite of 'heart', though, of course, 'heart' is technique too. A single blot on a paper by my friend Eugene Berman I instantly recognize as a Berman blot. What have I recognized—a style or a technique? Are they the same signature of the whole man? Stendhal (in the Roman Promenades) believed that style is 'the manner that each one has of saying the same thing'. But, obviously, no one says the same thing because the saying is also the thing. A technique or a style for saying something original does not exist *a priori*, it is created by the original saying itself. We sometimes say of a composer that he lacks technique. We say of Schumann, for example, that he did not have enough orchestral technique. But we do not believe that more technique would change the composer. 'Thought' is not one thing and 'technique' another, namely, the ability to transfer, 'express' or develop thoughts. We cannot say 'the technique of Bach' (I never say it), yet in every sense he had more of it than anyone; our extraneous meaning becomes ridiculous when we try to imagine the separation of Bach's musical substance and the making of it. Technique is not a teachable science, neither is it learning, nor scholarship, nor even the knowledge of how to do something. It is creation, and, being creation, it is new every time. There are other legitimate uses of the word, of course. Painters have water-colour and gouache techniques, for example, and there are technological meanings; we have techniques of bridge-building and even 'techniques for civilization'. In these senses one may talk of composing techniques—the writing of an academic fugue. But in my sense, the original composer is still his own and only technique. If I hear of a new composer's 'technical mastery' I am always interested in the composer (though critics employ the expression to mean 'but he hasn't got the more important thing'). Technical mastery has to be *of* something, it has to *be* something. And since we can recognize technical skill when we can recognize nothing else, it is the only manifestation of 'talent' I know of; up to a point technique and talent are the same. At present all of the arts, but especially music, are engaged in 'examinations of technique'. In my sense such an examination must be into the nature of art itself—an examination that is both perpetual and new every time—or it is nothing.[1]

R.C. Your music always has an element of repetition, of *ostinato*. What is the function of *ostinato*?

I.S. It is static—that is, anti-development; and sometimes we need

[1] In the case of my own music I know that my first works, the *Faune et Bergère* and the Symphony in E flat lack personality while at the same time they demonstrate definite technical ability with the musical materials. The *Faune* sounds like Wagner in places, like Tchaikovsky's *Romeo and Juliet* in other places (but never like Rimsky-Korsakov, which must have troubled that master), and like Stravinsky not at all, or only through thickly bespectacled hindsight.

a contradiction to development. However, it became a vitiating device and was at one time overemployed by many of us.

INSTRUMENTATION

R.C. What is good instrumentation?

I.S. When you are unaware that it *is* instrumentation. The word is a gloss. It pretends that one composes music and then orchestrates it. This is true, in fact, in the one sense that the only composers who can be orchestrators are those who write piano music which they transcribe for orchestra; and this might still be the practice of a good many composers, judging from the number of times I have been asked my opinion as to which instruments I think best for passages the composers play on the piano. As we know, real piano music, which is what these composers usually play, is the most difficult to instrumentate. Even Schoenberg, who was always an instrumental master (one could make a very useful anthology of instrumental practice in his music from the first song of op. 22 to *Von Heute auf Morgen* with its extraordinary percussion, piano and mandoline), even Schoenberg stumbled in trying to transfer Brahms's piano style to the orchestra (his arrangement of Brahms's G minor pianoforte quartet for orchestra), though his realization of the cadenza in the last movement with arpeggiated pizzicatos is a master stroke. It is not, generally, a good sign when the first thing we remark about a work is its instrumentation; and the composers we remark it of—Berlioz, Rimsky-Korsakov, Ravel—are not the best composers. Beethoven, the greatest orchestral master of all in our sense, is seldom praised for his instrumentation; his symphonies are too good music in every way and the orchestra is too integral a part of them. How silly it sounds to say of the trio of the Scherzo of the Eighth Symphony: 'What splendid instrumentation'—yet, what incomparable instrumental thought it is. Berlioz's reputation as an orchestrator has always seemed highly suspect to me. I was brought up on his music; it was played in the St. Petersburg of my student years as much as it has ever been played anywhere in the world,[1] so I dare say this to all the literary-minded people responsible for his revival. He was a great innovator, of course, and he had the perfect imagination of each new instrument he used, as well as the knowledge of its technique. But the music he had to instrumentate was often poorly constructed harmonically. No orchestral skill can hide the fact that Berlioz's basses are sometimes uncertain and the inner harmonic voices unclear. The problem of orchestral distribution is therefore insurmountable and balance is regulated superficially, by dynamics. This is in part why I prefer the small Berlioz to the grandiose.

Many composers still do not realize that our principal instrumental body today, the symphony orchestra, is the creation of harmonic-triadic music. They seem unaware that the growth of the wind instruments from two to three to four to five of a kind parallels a harmonic growth. It is extremely difficult to write polyphonically for this harmonic body, which is why Schoenberg in his polyphonic *Variations for Orchestra* is obliged to double, treble, and quadruple the *lines*. The bass,

[1] I remember a description of Berlioz by Rimsky-Korsakov who had met the French master after one of the famous Berlioz concerts in St. Petersburg in the late sixties. Rimsky-Korsakov, who was then twenty-three or twenty-four, had attended the concert with other young composers of the group. They saw Berlioz—in a tail-coat cut very short in the back, Rimsky said—conduct his own music and Beethoven's. Then they were shepherded backstage by Stassov, the patriarch of St. Petersburg musical life. They found a small man, Rimsky's words were 'a little white bird with pince-nez', shivering in a fur coat and huddled under a hot pipe which crossed the room just over his head. He addressed Rimsky very kindly: 'And you compose music too?', but kept his hands in his coat sleeves as in a muffler.

too, is extremely difficult to bring out acoustically and harmonically in the *Variations* because it is the lowest line, merely, and not bass-ic. Though the standard orchestra is not yet an anachronism, perhaps, it can no longer be used standardly except by anachronistic composers. Advances in instrumental technique are also modifying the use of the orchestra. We all compose for solo, virtuoso instrumentalists today, and our soloistic style is still being discovered. For example, harp parts were mostly glissandos or chords as recently as Ravel. The harp can glissando and arpeggiate *en masse*, but it can't play *en masse* as I have used it in my *Symphony in Three Movements*. And, for another example, we are just discovering the orchestral use of harmonics, especially bass harmonics (one of my favourite sounds incidentally; make your throat taut and open your mouth half an inch so that the skin of your neck becomes a drum-head, then flick your finger against it: that is the sound I mean).

At the beginning of my career the clarinet was considered incapable of long fast-tongue passages. I remember my Chopin instrumentations for *Les Sylphides* in Paris in 1910 and an ill-humoured clarinet player telling me after he had stumbled on a rapid staccato passage (the only way I could conceive Chopin's pianism): 'Monsieur, ce n'est pas une musique pour la clarinette.' What instruments do I like? I wish there were more good players for the bass clarinet and the contra-bass clarinet, for the alto trombone (of my *Threni* and Berg's *Altenberg Lieder*), for the guitar, the mandoline and the cymbalom. Do I dislike any instrument? Well, I am not very fond of the two most conspicuous instruments of the *Lulu* orchestra, the vibraphone and the alto saxophone. I do admit, however, that the vibraphone has amazing contrapuntal abilities; and the saxophone's juvenile-delinquent personality floating out over all the vast decadence of *Lulu* is the very apple of that opera's fascination.

About Composing and Compositions

R.C. Are you attracted by any new instruments—electric, oriental, exotic, jazz, whatever?

I.S. Of course, I am attracted by many non-standard orchestral instruments, percussion ones especially, but also stringed instruments like those Japanese ones I have heard in Los Angeles whose bridges are moved during the performance. And let us not forget the fact that traditional symphonic instruments like trumpet and trombone are not the same when played by jazz musicians. The latter people demonstrate greater variety in articulation and tone colour, and on some instruments, the trumpet for instance, they appear to be at home in a higher range than the symphonic player—the jazz trumpeter's high lip-trills. We neglect not only the instruments of other ethnographies, however, but those of our greatest European composer as well. This neglect is one reason why Bach's cantatas, which should be the centre of our repertoire, if we must have a repertoire, are comparatively unperformed. We don't have the instruments to play them. Bach had families where we have single instruments: trumpet families, trombone families, oboe families, families for all sorts of the strings. We have simplifications and greater resonance; where he had the lute, perhaps the most perfect and certainly the most personal instrument of all, we have the guitar. I myself prefer Bach's string orchestra with its gambas, its violino and 'cello piccolo, to our standard quartet in which the 'cello is not of the same family as the viola and bass. And, if oboes d'amore and da caccia were common I would compose for them. What incomparable instrumental writing is Bach's. You can smell the resin in his violin parts, taste the reeds in the oboes. I am always interested and attracted by new instruments (new to me) but until the present I have been more often astonished by the new resources imaginative composers are able to discover in 'old' instruments. An entry in Klee's *Tagebücher* says (under May 1913): 'Und das Mass ist noch nicht voll. Man führt sogar Schönberg auf, das tolle Melodram Pierrot Lunaire.' And not yet full now either. For example, Boulez's third piano sonata is quite as purely 'pianistic' as an *étude* by Debussy, yet it exploits varieties of touch (attack) untried by Debussy, and exposes in its harmonics a whole region of sound neglected until now. (These aspects of the piece are secondary, however, to the aspect of its form; always close to Mallarméan ideas of permutation, Boulez is now nearing a concept of form not unlike that of the idea of *Un Coup de Dés*; not only does the pagination of the score of his third piano sonata resemble the *Coup de Dés* 'score', but Mallarmé's own preface to the poem seems as well to describe the sonata: '. . . the fragmentary interruptions of a capital phrase introduced and continued . . . everything takes place by abridgement, hypothetically; one avoids the narration . . .'; Mallarmé thought he was borrowing ideas from music, of course, and would no doubt be surprised to know that sixty years later his poem had cross-pollinated the two arts; the recent publication of *Le Livre de Mallarmé*[1] with its startling diagrams of the mathematics of form must have been an uncanny confirmation to Boulez.)

Thus an 'old' instrument, the piano, interests me more than an Ondes Martinot, for instance, though this statement is in danger of giving the impression that I am thinking of instrumentalism as something apart from musical thoughts.

GESUALDO

R.C. What motivated you to compose new sextus and bassus parts for the lost ones in Gesualdo's motet *a sette*?

I.S. When I had written out the five existing parts in score, the

---

[1] By Jacques Scherer (Gallimard), the first study of Mallarmé's unpublished note-books and papers.

3. St. Petersburg, 1908

Stravinsky and his wife (extremes of picture) with Rimsky-Korsakov, and
Nadejda Rimsky-Korsakov with her fiancé Maximilian Steinberg

4. Clarens, 1913, the Hotel du Chatelard

The paintings to the left are Japanese (this is the period of Stravinsky's *Three Japanese Lyrics*). The large picture, extreme right just over the couch, is a Gauguin, given Stravinsky by 'an admirer of Petroushka' in Paris in 1912, but lost with all of Stravinsky's possessions in Oustiloug desire to complete Gesualdo's harmony, to soften certain of his *malheurs* became irresistible to me. One has to play the piece without any additions to understand me, and 'additions' is not an exact description; the existing material was only my starting point: from it I recomposed the whole. The existing parts impose definite limits in some cases, and very indefinite ones in others. But even if the existing parts did not rule out academic solutions, a knowledge of Gesualdo's other music would. I have not tried to guess 'what Gesualdo would have done', however—though I would like to see the original; I have even chosen solutions that I am sure are not Gesualdo's. And though Gesualdo's seconds and sevenths justify mine, I don't look at my work in that light. My parts are not attempts at reconstruction. I am in it as well as Gesualdo. The motet would have been unusual, I think, with or without me. Its form of nearly equal halves is unusual, and so is its consistent and complex polyphony: many of the motets employ a more simple chordal style, and with so many parts so close in range one would expect a treatment of that sort: Gesualdo's music is never dense. The bass part is unusual too. It is of bass-ic importance as it seldom is in Gesualdo. His madrigals are almost all top heavy and even in the motets and responses the bass rests more than any other part. I don't think I am reading myself into Gesualdo in this instance, though my musical thinking is always centred around the bass (the bass still functions as the harmonic root to me even in the music I am composing at present). But this motet which might be Gesualdo's ultimate opus would lead him to unusual things by the mere fact of its being his unique piece in seven parts.

(By the same reasoning I contend that the lost volume of six-voice madrigals contains more complex, more 'dissonant' music than the five-voice volumes, and the one reference we have to any of the madrigals in that book, to *Sei disposto*, bears me out; even his early six-part madrigal, *Donna, se m'ancidete,* has a great number of seconds besides those which are editors' errors.)

I would like to point out the very dramatic musical symbolization of the text that occurs at the dividing point of the form. The voices narrow to three (I am sure Gesualdo has done something similar), then at the words 'seven-fold grace of the paraclete' spread to seven full polyphonic parts.

I hope my little homage to Gesualdo and my own interest in that great musician will help excite the cupidity of other Gesualdines to the search for his lost work, the trio for the three famous ladies of Ferrara, the arias mentioned in Fontanelli's letters, and, above all, the six-part madrigals. This music must be in the Italian private libraries. (When Italy has been catalogued everything will reappear; recently Hotson, the Shakespearian, found a letter in an Orsini library describing an Orsini ancestor's impressions of a performance in Elizabeth's court of what must have been the first night of *Twelfth Night*.) Gesualdo was well related in Naples, in Ferrara, in Modena, in Urbino, even in Rome (his daughter married the Pope's nephew). Let us begin there.

TRANSLATION

R.C. No composer has been more directly concerned with the problems of musical texts sung in translation. Would you say something about the matter?

I.S. Let librettos and texts be published in translation, let synopses and arguments of plots be distributed in advance, let imaginations be appealed to, but do not change the sound and the stress of words that have been composed to precisely certain music at precisely certain places.

Anyway, the need to know 'what they are singing about' is not always satisfied by having it sung in one's own language, especially if that language happens to be English. There is a great lack of schools for singing English, in America at any rate; the casts of some American productions of opera-in-English do not all seem to be singing the same language. And 'meaning', the translator's *argument d'être*, is only one item. Translation changes the character of a work and destroys its cultural unity. If the original is verse, especially verse in a language rich in internal rhymes, it can only be adapted in a loose sense, not translated (except perhaps by Auden; Browning's lines beginning 'I could favour you with sundry touches', are a good example of just how extraordinary double rhymed verse sounds in English). Adaption implies translation of cultural locale, and results in what I mean by the destruction of cultural unity. For example, Italian prestos in English can hardly escape sounding like Gilbert and Sullivan, though this may be the fault of my Russian-born, naturalized-American ears and of my unfamiliarity with other periods of English opera (if after Purcell and before Britten there were other periods of English opera).

An example of translation destroying text and music occurs in the latter part of my *Renard*. The passage I am referring to —I call it a *pribaoutki*[1]—exploits a speed and an accentuation that are natural to Russian (each language has characteristic tempi which partly determine musical tempi and character). No translation of this passage can translate what I have done musically with the language. But there are many such instances in all of my Russian vocal music; I am so disturbed by them I prefer to hear those pieces in Russian or not at all. Fortunately Latin is still permitted to cross borders—at least no one has yet proposed to translate my *Oedipus*, my *Psalms*, my *Canticum*, and my *Mass*.

The presentation of works in their original language is a sign of a rich culture in my opinion. And, musically speaking, Babel is a blessing.

[1] A kind of droll song, sometimes to nonsense syllables, sometimes in part spoken. (I.S.)

2

ABOUT MUSICIANS AND OTHERS

ST. PETERSBURG

R.C. Do you remember your first attendance at a concert?

I.S. My first experience of a public musical performance was at the Mariinsky Theatre in St. Petersburg. My impressions of it are mixed with what I have been told, of course, but as a child of seven or eight I was taken to see *A Life for the Tsar*. We were given one of the official loges and I remember that it was adorned with gilt 'winged amours'. The spectacle of the theatre itself and of the audience bewildered me and my mother said later that as I watched the stage, carried away by the sound of the orchestra (perhaps the greatest thrill of my life was the sound of that first orchestra) I asked her, as in Tolstoy: 'Which one is the theatre?' I remember also that Nápravnik conducted the opera in white gloves.

The first concert of which I have any recollection was the occasion of a *première* of a symphony by Glazunov. I was nine or ten years old and at this time Glazunov was the heralded new composer. He *was* gifted with extraordinary powers of ear and memory, but it was going too far to assume from this that he must be a new Mozart: the sixteen-year-old prodigy was already a cut-and-dried academician. I was not inspired by this concert.

37

R.C. Were you impressed by any visiting foreign musicians in your student days in St. Petersburg?

I.S. In the early years of this century most of the distinguished foreign artists who came to St. Petersburg made calls of homage to Rimsky-Korsakov. I was in his home almost every day of 1903, 1904, and 1905, and therefore met many composers, conductors, and virtuosi there. Rimsky could speak French and English, the latter language having been acquired during his term as a naval officer, but he did not know German. As I spoke the language fluently from my childhood he sometimes asked me to translate for him and a German-speaking guest. I remember meeting the conductors Arthur Nikisch and Hans Richter in this way. The latter knew no word of any language but German, and Rimsky, with no German-speaking member of his family present had to send for me. When Richter saw me he scowled and asked: 'Wer ist dieser Jüngling?' I remember meeting Max Reger in those years, at a rehearsal I think. He and his music repulsed me in about equal measure. Alfredo Casella also came to Russia then, at the beginning of his career. I did not meet him at that time, but heard about him from Rimsky: 'A certain Alfredo Casella, an Italian musician, came to see me today. He brought me a complicated score of incredible size, his instrumentation of Balakirev's *Islamey* and asked me to comment on it and to advise him. What could one say about such a thing? I felt like a poor little child'—and saying so he seemed humiliated.

I remember seeing Mahler in St. Petersburg, too. His concert there was a triumph. Rimsky was still alive, I believe, but he wouldn't have attended because a work by Tchaikovsky was on the programme (I think it was *Manfred*, the dullest piece imaginable). Mahler also played some Wagner fragments and, if I remember correctly, a symphony of his own. Mahler impressed me greatly, himself and his conducting.

R.C. Would you describe Rimsky-Korsakov as a teacher?

I.S. He was a most unusual teacher. Though a professor at the St. Petersburg Conservatory himself, he advised me not to enter it; instead he made me the most precious gift of his unforgettable lessons (1903–6). These usually lasted a little more than an hour and took place twice a week. Schooling and training in orchestration was their main subject. He gave me Beethoven piano sonatas and quartets and Schubert marches to orchestrate, and sometimes his own music, the orchestration of which was not yet published. Then as I brought him the work I did, he showed me his own orchestra score, which he compared with mine, explaining his reasons for doing it differently.

In addition to these lessons I continued my contrapuntal exercises, but by myself, as I could not stand the boring lessons in harmony and counterpoint I had had with a former pupil of Rimsky-Korsakov.

R.C. What music of yours did Rimsky-Korsakov know? What did he say about it? What were his relations with new music: Debussy, Strauss, Scriabin?

I.S. When asked to go to a concert to hear Debussy's music he said: 'I have already heard it. I had better not go: I will start to get accustomed to it and finally like it.' He hated Richard Strauss but probably for the wrong reasons. His attitude towards Scriabin was different. He didn't like Scriabin's music at all, but to those people who were indignant about it his answer was: 'I like Scriabin's music very much.'

He knew well my Symphony in E flat, op. 1, dedicated to him, and also my vocal suite, *Faune et Bergère*, both performed in a concert arranged with his help and supervision. He had seen the manuscript of my *Scherzo Fantastique*, but his death prevented him from hearing it. He never complimented me; but he was always very close-mouthed and stingy in praising his pupils. But I was told by his friends after his death that he spoke with great praise of the *Scherzo* score.

R.C. Did you have Maeterlinck's *La Vie des Abeilles* in mind as a programme for your *Scherzo Fantastique*?

I.S. No, I wrote the *Scherzo* as a piece of 'pure' symphonic music. The bees were a choreographer's idea as, later, the bee-like creatures of the ballet (to my string concerto in D), *The Cage*, were Mr. Robbins's. I have always been fascinated by bees, awed by them after von Fritsch's book, and terrified after my friend Gerald Heard's *Is another World Watching*, but I have never attempted to evoke them in my work (as, indeed, what pupil of the composer of the *Flight of the Bumble Bee* would?) nor have I been influenced by them except that, defying Galen's advice to elderly people (to Marcus Aurelius?) I continue to eat a daily diet of honey.

Maeterlinck's bees nearly gave me serious trouble, however. One morning in Morges I received a startling letter from him, accusing me of intent to cheat and fraud. My *Scherzo* had been entitled *Les Abeilles*—anyone's title, after all—and made the subject of a ballet then performing at the Paris Grand Opera (1917). *Les Abeilles* was unauthorized by me and, of course, I had not seen it; but Maeterlinck's name was mentioned in the programme. The affair was settled and, finally, some bad literature about bees was published on the fly-leaf of my score, to satisfy my publisher, who thought a 'story' would help to sell the music. I regretted the incident with Maeterlinck because I had considerable respect for him in Russian translation.

Sometime later I recounted this episode to Paul Claudel. Claudel considered Maeterlinck to have been unusually polite to me: 'He often starts suits against people who say *bonjour* to him. You were lucky not to have been sued for the 'bird' part of the *Firebird*, since Maeterlinck had written the *Bluebird* first.'[1]

[1] Since writing this I have conducted three performances of the

About Musicians and Others

This bee-ology reminds me of Rachmaninov, of all people, for the last time I saw that awesome man he had come to my house in Hollywood bearing me the gift of a pail of honey. I was not especially friendly with Rachmaninov at the time, nor, I think, was anyone else: social relations with a man of Rachmaninov's temperament require more perseverance than I can afford: he was merely bringing me honey. It is curious, however, that I should meet him not in Russia, though I often heard him perform there in my youth, nor later when we were neighbours in Switzerland, but in Hollywood.

Some people achieve a kind of immortality just by the totality with which they do or do not possess some quality or characteristic. Rachmaninov's immortalizing totality was his scowl. He was a six-and-a-half-foot-tall scowl.

I suppose my conversations with him, or rather, with his wife, for he was always silent, were typical:

Scherzo ('whether or not it is "Fantastique" is up to us to decide', one French critic wrote after its première in St. Petersburg under the baton of Alexander Ziloti) and was surprised to find that the music did not embarrass me. The orchestra 'sounds', the music is light in a way that is rare in compositions of the period, and there are one or two quite good ideas in it such as the flute and violin music at no. 63 and the chromatic movement of the last page. Of course the phrases are all four plus four plus four, which is monotonous, and, hearing it again, I was sorry that I did not more exploit the alto flute. It is a promising opus three, though.

I see now that I did take something from Rimsky's Bumblebee (numbers 49–50 in the score), but the *Scherzo* owes much more to Mendelssohn by way of Tchaikovsky than to Rimsky-Korsakov.

The progress of instrumental technique was illustrated to me by these recent performances in an interesting detail. The original score—written more than fifty years ago—employs three harps. I remember very well how difficult all three parts were for the harpists in St. Petersburg in 1908. In 1930 I reduced the three parts to two for a new edition of the orchestral material. Now I see that with a few adjustments the same music can be performed by one player, so much quicker are harpists at their pedals.

Mme Rachmaninov: 'What is the first thing you do when you rise in the morning?' (This could have been indiscreet, but not if you had seen how it was asked.)

Myself: 'For fifteen minutes I do exercises taught me by a Hungarian gymnast and Kneipp Kur maniac, or, rather, I did them until I learned that the Hungarian had died very young and very suddenly, then I stand on my head, then I take a shower.'

Mme Rachmaninov: 'You see, Serge, *Stravinsky* takes showers. How extraordinary. Do you still say you are afraid of them? And you heard Stravinsky say that he exercises? What do you think of that? Shame on you who will hardly take a walk.'

Rachmaninov: (Silence.)

I remember Rachmaninov's earliest compositions. They were 'water-colours', songs and piano pieces freshly influenced by Tchaikovsky. Then at twenty-five he turned to 'oils' and became a very old composer indeed. Do not expect me to spit on him for that, however: he was, as I have said, an awesome man, and besides, there are too many others to be spat upon before him. As I think about him, his silence looms as a noble contrast to the self-approbations which are the only conversation of all performing and most other musicians. And, he was the only pianist I have ever seen who did not grimace. That is a great deal.

R.C. When you were a pupil of Rimsky-Korsakov, did you esteem Tchaikovsky as much as you did later, in the twenties and thirties?

I.S. Then as later in my life I was annoyed by the too frequent vulgarity of his music—annoyed in the same measure as I enjoyed the real freshness of Tchaikovsky's talent (and his instrumental inventiveness), especially when I compared it with the stale naturalism and amateurism of the 'Five' (Borodin, Rimsky-Korsakov, Cui, Balakirev, and Mussorgsky).

R.C. What was Rimsky-Korsakov's attitude to Brahms and when did you yourself first encounter Brahms's music?

I.S. I remember reading the notice of Brahms's death in *New Time* (the St. Petersburg conservative newspaper; I subscribed to it for Rozanov's articles) and the impression it made on me. I know that at least three years prior to it I had played quartets and symphonies by the Hamburg master.

Brahms was the discovery of my 'uncle' Alexander Ielatchich, husband of my mother's sister, Sophie. This gentleman who had an important role in my early development was a civil service general and a wealthy man. He was a passionate musical amateur who would spend days at a time playing the piano. Two of his five sons were musical, too, and one of them or myself was always playing four-hand music with him. I remember going through a Brahms quartet with him this way in my twelfth year. Uncle Alexander was an admirer of Mussorgsky and as such he had little use for Rimsky-Korsakov. His house was just around the corner from Rimsky's, however, and I would often go from one to the other, finding it difficult to keep a balance between them.

Rimsky did not like Brahms. He was no Wagnerite either, but his admiration for Liszt kept him on the Wagner–Liszt side of the partisanship.

R.C. What opinion did you have of Mussorgsky when you were Rimsky-Korsakov's student? Do you remember anything your father may have said about him? How do you consider him today?

I.S. I have very little to say about Mussorgsky in connection with my student years under Rimsky-Korsakov. At that time, being influenced by the master who recomposed almost the whole work of Mussorgsky, I repeated what was usually said about his 'big talent' and 'poor musicianship', and about the 'important services' rendered by Rimsky to his 'embarrassing' and 'unpresentable' scores. Very soon I realized the partiality of this kind of mind, however, and changed my attitude toward Mussorgsky. This was before my contact with the French composers who, of course, were all fiercely opposed to Rimsky's 'transcriptions'. It was too obvious, even to an influenced mind, that Rimsky's Meyerbeerization of Mussorgsky's 'technically imperfect' music could no longer be tolerated.

As to my own feeling (although I have little contact with Mussorgsky's music today) I think that in spite of his limited technical means and 'awkward writing' his original scores always show infinitely more true musical interest and genuine intuition than the 'perfection' of Rimsky's arrangements. My parents often told me that Mussorgsky was a connoisseur of Italian operatic music and that he accompanied concert singers in it extremely well. They also said that Mussorgsky's manners were always ceremonious and that he was the most fastidious of men in his personal relations. He was a frequent guest in our house at St. Petersburg.

R.C. You often conduct Glinka's overtures. Have you always been fond of his music?

I.S. Glinka was the Russian musical hero of my childhood. He was always *sans reproche* and this is the way I still think of him. His music is minor, of course, but he is not; all music in Russia stems from him. In 1906, shortly after my marriage, I went with my wife and Nikolsky, my civics professor at the University of St. Petersburg, to pay a visit of respect to Glinka's sister, Ludmilla Shestakova. An old lady of ninety-two or ninety-three, she was surrounded by servants almost as old as herself and she did not attempt to get up from her chair.

She had been the wife of an admiral and one addressed her as 'Your Excellency'. I was thrilled to meet her because she had been very close to Glinka. She talked to me about Glinka, about my late father, whom she had known very well, about the Cui-Dargomizhsky circle and its rabid anti-Wagnerism. Afterwards as a memento of my visit she sent me a silver leaf of edelweiss.

R.C. Did you ever meet Balakirev?

I.S. I saw him once, standing with his pupil, Liapunov, at a concert in the St. Petersburg Conservatory. He was a large man, bald, with a Kalmuck head and the shrewd, sharp-eyed look of Lenin. He was not greatly admired musically at this time —it was 1904 or 1905—and, politically, because of his orthodoxy, the liberals considered him a hypocrite. His reputation as a pianist was firmly established by numerous pupils, however, all of them, like Balakirev himself, ardent Lisztians; whereas Rimsky-Korsakov kept a portrait of Wagner over his desk, Balakirev had one of Liszt. I pitied Balakirev because he suffered from cruel fits of depression.

R.C. You do not mention in your autobiography whether you attended Rimsky-Korsakov's funeral?

I.S. I did not mention it because it was one of the unhappiest days of my life. But I was there and I will remember Rimsky in his coffin as long as memory is. He looked so very beautiful I could not help crying. His widow, seeing me, came up to me and said: 'Why so unhappy? We still have Glazunov.' It was the cruellest remark I have ever heard and I have never hated again as I did in that moment.

DIAGHILEV

R.C. What were Diaghilev's powers of musical judgment? What, for example, was his response to *Le Sacre du Printemps* when he first heard it?

I.S. Diaghilev did not have so much a good musical judgment as an immense flair for recognizing the potentiality of success in a piece of music or work of art in general. In spite of his surprise when I played him the beginning of the *Sacre* (*Les Augures Printanières*) at the piano, in spite of his at first ironic attitude to the long line of repeated chords, he quickly realized that the reason was something other than my inability to compose more diversified music; he realized at once the seriousness of my new musical speech, its importance and the advantage of capitalizing on it. That, it seems to me, is what he thought on first hearing the *Sacre*.

R.C. Was the musical performance of the first *Sacre du Printemps* reasonably correct? Do you recall anything more about that night of 29th May 1913, beyond what you have already written?

I.S. I was sitting in the fourth or fifth row on the right and the image of Monteux's back is more vivid in my mind today than the picture of the stage. He stood there apparently impervious and as nerveless as a crocodile. It is still almost incredible to me that he actually brought the orchestra through to the end. I left my seat when the heavy noises began —light noise had started from the very beginning—and went backstage behind Nijinsky in the right wing. Nijinsky stood on a chair, just out of view of the audience, shouting numbers to the dancers. I wondered what on earth these numbers had to do with the music for there are no 'thirteens' and 'seventeens' in the metrical scheme of the score.

From what I heard of the musical performance it was not bad. Sixteen full rehearsals had given the orchestra at least some security. After the 'performance' we were excited, angry, disgusted, and . . . happy. I went with Diaghilev and Nijinsky to a restaurant. So far from weeping and reciting Pushkin in the Bois de Boulogne as the legend is, Diaghilev's only comment was: 'Exactly what I wanted.' He certainly looked contented. No one could have been quicker to understand the publicity value and he immediately understood the good thing that had happened in that respect. Quite probably he had already thought about the possibility of such a scandal when I first played him the score, months before, in the east corner ground room of the Grand Hotel in Venice.

R.C. Had you ever planned a Russian 'liturgical ballet'? If so, did any of it become *Les Noces*?

I.S. No, that 'liturgical ballet' was entirely Diaghilev's idea. He knew that a Russian church spectacle in a Paris theatre would be enormously successful. He had wonderful ikons and costumes he wished to show and he kept pestering me to give him music. Diaghilev was not really religious, not really a believer, but only a deeply superstitious man. He wasn't at all shocked by the idea of the church in the theatre. I began to conceive *Les Noces*, and its form was already clear in my mind, from about the beginning of 1914. At the time of Sarajevo I was in Clarens. I needed Kireievsky's book of Russian folk poetry, from which I had made my libretto, and I determined to go to Kiev which was the only place where I knew I could get it. I took the train to Oustiloug, our summer home in Volhynia, in July 1914. After a few days there I went on to Warsaw and Kiev, where I found the book. I regret that on this last trip, my last view of Russia, I did not see the Vydubitsky Monastery which I knew and loved. On the return trip the border police were already very tense. I arrived in Switzerland only a few days before the war—thanking my stars. Incidentally, Kireievsky had asked Pushkin to send him his collection of folk verse and Pushkin sent him some verses with a note reading: 'Some of these are my own verses; can you tell the difference?' Kireievsky could not, and took them all for his book, so perhaps a line of Pushkin's is in *Les Noces*.

DEBUSSY

R.C. Of your early contemporaries, to whom do you owe the most? Debussy? Do you think Debussy changed from his contact with you?

I.S. I was handicapped in my earliest years by influences that restrained the growth of my composer's technique. I refer to the St. Petersburg Conservatory's formalism, from which, however—and fortunately—I was soon free. But the musicians of my generation and I myself owe the most to Debussy.

I don't think there was a change in Debussy as a result of our contact. After reading his friendly and commendatory letters to me (he liked *Petroushka* very much) I was puzzled to find quite a different feeling concerning my music in some of his letters to his musical friends of the same period. Was it duplicity, or was he annoyed at his incapacity to digest the music of the *Sacre* when the younger generation enthusiastically voted for it? This is difficult to judge now at a distance of more than forty years.

LETTERS FROM DEBUSSY

1

Saturday, 10th April 1913
80 avenue de Bois de Boulogne

(Letter sent to me in Oustiloug.)

Dear Friend,

Thanks to you I have passed an enjoyable Easter vacation in the company of Petroushka, the terrible Moor, and the delicious Ballerina. I can imagine that you spent incomparable moments with the three puppets . . . and I don't know many things more valuable than the section you call 'Tour de passe-passe'. . . . There is in it a kind of sonorous magic, a mysterious transformation of mechanical souls which be-

5. Leysin (Canton de Vaud), 1914
The final scenes of *Le Rossignol* were composed here

6. Morges (Switzerland), 1915
Stravinsky with his sons, Soulima (b. 1910, on his back) and Theodore
(b. 1907), and his daughter (Ludmilla, 1909–1938)

come human by a spell of which, until now, you seem to be the unique inventor.

Finally, there is an orchestral infallibility that I have found only in *Parsifal*. You will understand what I mean, of course. You will go much further than *Petroushka*, it is certain, but you can be proud already of the achievement of this work.

I am sorry, please accept my belated thanks in acknowledging your kind gift. But the dedication gives me much too high a place in the mastery of that music which we both serve with the same disinterested zeal. . . . Unhappily, at this time, I was surrounded with sick people! especially my wife who has been suffering for many long days. . . . I even had to be the 'man about the house' and I will admit to you at once that I have no talent for it.

Since the good idea of performing you again is talked about, I look forward with pleasure to see you soon here.

Please don't forget the way to my house where everyone is anxious to see you.

Very affectionately your
CLAUDE DEBUSSY

2

Paris, 8th November 1913

Don't fall to the ground, Dear Friend, it is only me! ! ! Of course, if we begin, you wishing to understand and I to explain why I haven't written yet, our hair will fall out.

And then, something marvellous is happening here: at least once a day everyone talks about you. Your friend Chouchou[1] has composed a fantasy on *Petroushka* which would make tigers roar. . . . I have threatened her with torture, but she goes on, insisting that you will 'find it very beautiful'. So, how could you suppose that we are not thinking of you?

---

[1] Debussy's daughter Emma-Claude, who died one year after her father.

Our reading at the piano of *Le Sacre du Printemps*, at Laloy's[1] house, is always present in my mind. It haunts me like a beautiful nightmare and I try, in vain, to reinvoke the terrific impression.

That is why I wait for the stage performance like a greedy child impatient for promised sweets.

As soon as I have a good proof copy of *Jeux* I will send it to you. . . . I would love to have your opinion on this 'badinage in three parts'. While speaking of *Jeux*, you were surprised that I chose this title to which you preferred *The Park*. I beg you to believe that *Jeux* is better, first because it is more appropriate, and then because it more nearly invokes the 'horrors' that occur among these three characters.[2]

When are you coming to Paris so one may at last play good music?

Very affectionately from us three to you and your wife.

Your very old friend,

CLAUDE DEBUSSY

3

15th May 1913

Dear Friend,

My telephone doesn't work and I fear you have tried to call without success. If you have seen Nijinsky and if he signed the papers please give them to the chauffeur. It is urgent that they

[1] Which Louis Laloy, the critic, incorrectly attributes to the spring of 1913. What most impressed me at the time and what is still most memorable from the occasion of the sight reading of *Le Sacre* was Debussy's brilliant piano playing. Recently, while listening to his *En blanc et noir* (one of which pieces is dedicated to me) I was struck by the way in which the extraordinary quality of this pianism had directed the thought of Debussy the composer.

[2] Debussy was in close contact with me during the composition of *Jeux* and he frequently consulted me about problems of orchestration. I still consider *Jeux* as an *orchestral* masterpiece, though I think some of the music is 'trop Lalique'.

are at the Société des Auteurs before five o'clock. Thank you, your old Debussy.

(This note brought by Debussy's chauffeur refers to forms from the Société des Auteurs Debussy had given me to give Nijinsky the co-stage author of *Jeux*. I was seeing Nijinsky every day at this time and Debussy was only sure of reaching him through me.)

4

Paris, 18th August 1913

Dear Old Stravinsky,

Excuse me for being late in thanking you for a work whose dedication is priceless to me.[1] I have been taken with an attack of 'expulsive gingivitis'. It is ugly and dangerous and one could wake up in the morning to discover one's teeth falling out. Then, of course, they could be strung into a necklace. Perhaps this is not much consolation?

The music from the *Roi des Étoiles* is still extraordinary. It is probably Plato's 'harmony of the eternal spheres' (but don't ask me which page of his). And, except on Sirius or Aldebaran, I do not foresee performances of this 'cantata for planets'. As for our more modest Earth, a performance would be lost in the abyss.

I hope that you have recovered. Take care, music needs you. Kindly convey my respects to your charming mother and best wishes to your wife.

Your old faithful

CLAUDE DEBUSSY

---

[1] I had dedicated my short cantata *Le Roi des Étoiles* (1911) to Debussy. He was obviously puzzled by the music, and nearly right in predicting it to be unperformable—it has had only a few performances in very recent years and remains in one sense my most 'radical' and difficult composition.

5

Dear Stravinsky,

Because one still belongs to certain traditions, one wonders why one's letter is not answered . . . ! But the value of the music I have received[1] is more important because it contains something affirmative and victorious. Naturally, people who are a little bit embarrassed by your growing mastery have not neglected to spread very discordant rumours—and if you are not already dead it is not their fault. I have never believed in a rumour—is it necessary to tell you this?—No! Also, it is not necessary to tell you of the joy I had to see my name associated with a very beautiful thing that with the passage of time will be more beautiful still.

For me, who descend the other slope of the hill but keep, however, an intense passion for music, for me it is a special satisfaction to tell you how much you have enlarged the boundaries of the permissible in the empire of sound.

Forgive me for using these pompous words, but they exactly express my thought.

You have probably heard about the melancholy end of the Théâtre des Champs Élysées? It is really a pity that the only place in Paris where one had started to play music honestly could not be successful. May I ask you dear friend, what you propose to do about it? I saw Diaghilev at *Boris Godunov*, the only performance it had, and he said nothing. . . . If you can give me some news without being indiscreet, do not hesitate. In any case are you coming to Paris? 'How many questions' I hear you saying. . . . If you are annoyed to answer. . . .

This very moment I received your postcard—and I see by it, dear friend, that you never received my letter. It is very regettable for me—you are probably very angry with me. Perhaps I wrote the address incorrectly. And also, Oustiloug is so

---

[1] I had sent him the score of *Le Sacre du Printemps*.

far away. I will not go to Lausanne—for some complicated reasons which are of no interest to you. This is one more reason for you to come to Paris—to have the joy of seeing each other.

Know that I am going to Moscow the first of December. I gather you will not be there? Believe me that for this reason my journey will be a little more painful. I wrote to Kussevitsky asking him for some necessary information—he does not answer.

As for the 'Société de la Musique Actuelle' I want to do my best to be agreeable and to thank them for the honour they want to bestow on me. Only I don't know if I will have enough time to stay for the concert.

My wife and Chouchou send you their affectionate thoughts and ask you not to forget to give the same to your wife.

Always your old devoted

CLAUDE DEBUSSY

6

(postcard)

Paris, 17 November 1913

Dear Stravinsky, You have acquired the habit since childhood to play with the calendar and I confess that your last card confused me. At the same time I received a telegram from Kussevitsky telling me that I am expected in Moscow December 3 (new style). As the concert in St. Petersburg is the 10th you can see that I will not have time to do anything. Are you recovered from your cold? I heartily hope so. If you have nothing better to do I advise you to go to Moscow. It is a marvellous city and you probably don't know it very well. You will meet there Claude Debussy, French musician, who loves you very much.

Affectionately, CLAUDE DEBUSSY

7

Paris, 24th October 1915

First of all, dearest friend, it is a joy to hear from you at last. . . . I had some news from your friends, who, I don't know why, kept the state of your health and your residence a mystery.

We are all doing somewhat better, or in other words we are like the majority of the French people. We have our share of sorrows, of spiritual and domestic difficulties. But this is natural now that Europe and the rest of the world think it necessary to participate in this tragic 'concert'. Why don't the inhabitants of Mars join the fray?

As you wrote to me: 'They will be unable to make us join their madness.' All the same there is something higher than brute force; to 'close the windows' on beauty is against reason and destroys the true meaning of life.

But one must open one's eyes and ears to other sounds when the noise of the cannon has subsided! The world must be rid of this bad seed. We have all to kill the microbes of false grandeur, of organized ugliness, which we did not always realize was simply weakness.

You will be needed in the war against those other, and just as mortal, gases for which there are no masks.

Dear Stravinsky, you are a great artist. Be with all your strength a great Russian artist. It is so wonderful to be of one's country, to be attached to one's soil like the humblest of peasants! And when the foreigner treads upon it how bitter all the nonsense about internationalism seems.

In these last years, when I smelled 'austro-boches' miasma in art, I wished for more authority to shout my worries, warn of the dangers we so credulously approached. Did no one suspect these people of plotting the destruction of our art as they had prepared the destruction of our countries? And this ancient national hate that will end only with the last German! But will there ever be a 'last German'? For I am convinced that German soldiers beget German soldiers.

As for *Nocturnes*, Doret (the Swiss composer) is right, I made many modifications. Unhappily, they are published by a publisher, Fromont, Colysée Street, with whom I am no more associated. Another trouble is that there are no more copyists, at this moment, capable of doing this delicate work. I shall search further and try to find a way to satisfy M. Ansermet.

It must be confessed that music is in a bad situation here.... It only serves charitable purposes, and we must not blame it for that. I remained here for more than a year without being able to write any music. Only during these last three months spent at the seaside with friends have I recovered the faculty of musical thinking. Unless one is personally involved in it, war is a state of mind contradictory to thought. That olympian egotist Goethe is the only one who could work, it is said, the day the French army came into Weimar. . . . Then there was Pythagoras killed by a soldier at the moment when he was going to solve God knows what problem?

Recently I have written nothing but pure music, twelve piano *études* and two sonatas for different instruments, in our old form which, very graciously, did not impose any tetralogical auditory efforts.

And you, dear friend, what have you been doing? Don't for heaven's sake think you have to answer that question. I ask not out of vulgar curiosity but in pure affection.

And your wife and children? Have you worries about them?

My wife suffered badly from her eyes and from an unbearable neuralgia-rheumatism. Chouchou has a cold; she makes it into something very serious by the attention she pays to her little person.

It is very difficult to know when we will see each other and so we have only the weak resource of 'words'. . . . Well, believe me your always devoted old

CLAUDE DEBUSSY

All our affectionate thoughts to your dear family. I have received news from the 'Société des Auteurs' saying that you had chosen me as godfather for your entry in that society. I thank you.

JACQUES RIVIÈRE

R.C. You have said that Jacques Rivière, as editor of the *Nouvelle Revue Française*, was the first critic to have had an intuition about your music. What were his musical capabilities?

I.S. At this distance I am not really able to answer that, for though I knew Rivière well before the 1914 war I never saw him again after it and in forty-five years memories change colour. However, I can say that at the time I considered his criticism of my ballets to be literary, inspired more by the whole spectacle than by my music. He *was* musical, certainly, and his musical tastes were genuine and cultivated, but whether he was capable of following the musical argument of *Le Sacre du Printemps* I can no longer judge.

I remember Jacques Rivière as a tall, blond, intellectually energetic youth, a passionate balletomane and at the same time a man with a deep religious vocation. He came to Geneva from time to time when I lived there and these meetings with him always afforded me much pleasure. He lived in semi-retirement after the war, his health ruined by his years as a prisoner of the Germans, and he died still young, a broken man.

Re-reading his letters I am struck (*a*) by the malady of the French about theatre tickets; they will do absolutely anything to get tickets except *buy* them; if Rivière was so 'vivement' interested in the *Nightingale* why didn't he go to the *guichet* and exchange a few francs for them?; and (*b*) by the evidence in the fourth letter of how quickly fashion had turned against Debussy in the year after his death.

LETTERS FROM JACQUES RIVIÈRE

1

Editions de la Nouvelle Revue Française
35 and 37 Rue Madame, Paris
4th February 1914

My dear Stravinsky,

I am rather late in telling you how grateful I am. But I have been near you in my thoughts all these days as I have started to put on paper some ideas about the *Nightingale*.[1]

You were very kind to have sent these two cards to Galli-mard and to me. They gave us great pleasure.

I intend to come to your concert[2] Saturday and perhaps I will be able to shake your hand.

Believe me, my dear Stravinsky . . .

JACQUES RIVIÈRE

[1] I was in Leysin in January 1914 completing the *Nightingale*. Cocteau came there in the hope of persuading me to collaborate with him on a work to be called *David*, and Diaghilev followed him a few days later with the express intention of discouraging this same project. Diaghilev-Cocteau relations were not ideal at the time, anyway, as Diaghilev could not stand Cocteau's fondness for Nijinsky, but Diaghilev's excuse for the trip was the *Nightingale*. Until then he had ignored the existence of this opera (out of jealousy, it had been commissioned by a Moscow theatre) but recently the people who were to produce it had declared bankruptcy and he was now very interested: I had been paid by them (10,000 rubles, a huge sum of money for 1909) and he could have the opera for nothing. We returned to Paris where I played the *Nightingale* for Ravel and a group of friends. Among these was Jacques Rivière.

[2] I have no recollection of this concert.

2

Paris, 25th May 1914

Dear Sir,

Is it extremely indiscreet of me to ask you for two or three tickets to the *première* of the *Nightingale*? I take this liberty only because yesterday evening I heard that a large number of complimentary tickets are available. You may well imagine how much I want my wife to hear this work from which I myself anticipate so much pleasure.[1] But if it is impossible please do not hesitate to refuse me.[2] If you are able to get tickets only for the second performance I certainly will not refuse them though of course I would prefer to attend the *première*. Yesterday I again heard the music of *Petroushka*, and with profound emotion. I beg you, dear sir, to excuse my importunity and to believe in my friendship and sympathy.

JACQUES RIVIÈRE
15 rue Froidevaux, Paris XIV

3

Paris, May 1914

Dear Sir,

You are exceedingly kind to have thought of me and I thank you with all my heart. Unfortunately, I had gone away the moment your telegram arrived and this is the reason why I did not use the place you offered me in your loge. I succeeded in entering the Opera, however, but the conditions under which I heard the *Nightingale* were so unfavourable that I am not yet able to judge it well. But already I see that it promises me beautiful discoveries for the next performances.

Again thank you, dear sir, and please believe in my admiration and my sympathy.

JACQUES RIVIÈRE

[1] He had attended some of the rehearsals.
[2] *Sic.*

4

La Nouvelle Revue Française
35 and 37 Rue Madame, Paris
6th April 1919

My dear Stravinsky,

I asked Auberjonois[1] to tell you how much pleasure your letter gave me. Probably he has done so, but I thank you·most sincerely again.

It is another matter I want to talk to you about today, however. Perhaps you already know that my friends have decided to entrust me with the direction of the *Nouvelle Revue Française*, which will reappear June 1. It is an honour of which I am very proud, but it is also a heavy burden and a source of grave preoccupations.

I intend to direct the attention of the magazine to the anti-impressionist, anti-symbolist, and anti-Debussy movements that are becoming more and more precise and threatening to take the form and force of a vast new current. I would be extremely happy if you think you could show us in an article (you may decide the dimensions of it yourself) your present ideas on music and the meaning of the work you are devoting yourself to at the moment.

But do not think you have been forgotten here. Everyone I see talks about you constantly. The influence of *Petroushka* and *Sacre* and even of your recent works on the younger musicians is obvious. An article by you will be read with curiosity and sympathy everywhere in the world. To make it easier for you, you could write it in Russian. If you have no one around to translate it, I think I can take charge of that, with the condition that the manuscript you send me is very legibly written. Of course, I will submit my translation to you for rectification.

[1] René Auberjonois, the late Swiss painter, who designed the first production of my *L'Histoire du Soldat*.

I do not need to tell you that without promising mountains of gold, I will assure you of our best possible fee for your work.

Please forgive me for having fulfilled only one part of the requests you charged me with when we last saw each other in Geneva. Most of the people you asked me to see were not in Paris when I arrived there, however, and I myself was so long absent that by the time I finally returned some of the requests were out of date.

I will confidently await your answer hoping that it will not be otherwise than favourable, and with this conviction I beg you my dear Stravinsky to believe in my deepest friendship.

JACQUES RIVIÈRE

PS.—Do not forget to give my best wishes to Ramuz[1] and Auberjonois. If it will be difficult for you to send me your manuscript because of the Russian, please inform me and I will ask someone I know at the Foreign Affairs Office to facilitate the sending, and obtain the necessary authorization for you.

5

Paris, 21st April 1919

My dear Stravinsky,

Of course your letter was disappointing as it deprives me of your collaboration; but it delighted me also because I think as you do, that a real creator should not lose his time discoursing about the tendencies and consequences of his art. His work must be self-explanatory. However, if one day the desire overtakes you to write not about yourself, but about others, about Debussy for instance, or Russian contemporary

---

[1] C. F. Ramuz, the late Swiss novelist and co-librettist with me of *L'Histoire du Soldat.*

music, or some other subject, then think about me and do not forget that our pages are always open to you.

With friendship, your

JACQUES RIVIÈRE

P.S. What is this new 'Suite from the *Firebird*', a ballet?[1]

RAVEL

R.C. Have you any notion where the manuscript of yours and Ravel's instrumentation of *Khovanshchina* might be?

I.S. I left it in Oustiloug on my last trip to Russia and therefore assume it to be lost or destroyed. (I wish someone travelling in Volhynia and passing through Oustiloug would investigate whether my house still stands; not long ago some kind person sent me a photograph of it but did not mention whether it had survived the Nazi invasion and I could not tell if the photo was pre- or post-war.) However, I feel certain that Bessel had already engraved it in Russia just before the (1914) war. The plates should exist, therefore, with the inheritors of Bessel's Russian firm. I remember a money struggle with Bessel who said we were demanding too much and argued that 'Mussorgsky received only a fraction of what you are asking'.

I replied that because they had given Mussorgsky precisely nothing, because they had succeeded in starving the poor man, was the greater reason to give us more.

The idea of asking Ravel to collaborate with me on an instrumentation of *Khovanshchina* was mine. I was afraid not to be ready for the spring season of 1913 and I needed help. Unfortunately, however, Diaghilev cared less about establishing a good instrumentation of the opera and rescuing it from Rimsky-Korsakov than about our version as a new vehicle for Chaliapin. That idiot from every non-vocal point

---

[1] My 1919 version of the *Firebird* suite, which I think he might have guessed.

of view, and from some of these, could not realize the value of such an instrumentation. He declined to sing and the project was abandoned, though we had already done considerable work. I orchestrated Shaklovity's famous and banal aria, the final chorus and some other music I no longer remember. Mussorgsky had only sketched, really only projected, the final chorus; I began with Mussorgsky's original and composed it from Mussorgsky ignoring Rimsky-Korsakov.

Ravel came to Clarens to live with me and we worked together there in March–April 1913. At that same time also, I composed my *Three Japanese Lyrics* and Ravel his *Trois Poèmes de Mallarmé* which I still prefer to any music of his. I remember an excursion I made with Ravel from Clarens to Varese, near Lago Maggiore, to buy Varese paper. The town was very crowded and we could not find two hotel rooms or even two beds, so we slept together in one.

Ravel? When I think of him, for example in relation to Satie, he appears quite ordinary. His musical judgment was very acute, however, and I would say that he was the only musician who immediately understood *Le Sacre du Printemps*. He was dry and reserved and sometimes little darts were hidden in his remarks, but he was always a very good friend to me. He drove a truck or ambulance in the war, as you know, and I admired him for it because at his age and with his name he could have had an easier place—or done nothing. He looked rather pathetic in his uniform; so small, he was two or three inches smaller than I am.

I think Ravel knew when he went into the hospital for his last operation that he would go to sleep for the last time. He said to me: 'They can do what they want with my cranium as long as the ether works.' It didn't work, however, and the poor man felt the incision. I did not visit him in this hospital and my last view of him was in a funeral home. The top part of his skull was still bandaged. His final years were cruel, for he was gradually losing his memory and some of his co-ordinating powers, and, he was, of course, quite aware of it. Gogol died screaming and Diaghilev died laughing (and singing *La Bohème* which he loved genuinely and as much as any music), but Ravel died gradually. That is the worst.

LETTERS FROM RAVEL

1

Comarques, Thorpe-Le-Soken
13th December 1913

Vieux—it's a long time since I've had any sensational news about your health. Three weeks ago I heard about your sudden death, but was not stricken by it as the same morning we received a postcard from you.

Delage[1] surely told you that your 'Japanese' will be performed January 14th together with his 'Hindus' and my 'Mallarméans'. . . . We count on your presence.

I will be in London in three days and hope to hear talk about the *Sacre*.

And the *Nightingale*, will he soon sing?

My respectful compliments to Mme Stravinsky, kiss the children, and believe in the affection of your devoted

MAURICE RAVEL

2

St. Jean de Luz
14th February 1914

Dear Igor,

I hear from Casella[2] that Madame Stravinsky went to Leysin.

[1] Maurice Delage, the composer, a good friend to me at this time. My *Three Japanese Lyrics* are dedicated to Maurice Delage, Florent Schmitt, and Maurice Ravel respectively.

[2] The composer, Alfredo Casella, and his wife were living in Paris at this time.

I hope it is only a precaution. I beg you, reassure me by a word.

I have taken refuge here in the country of my birthplace to work, as work was becoming quite impossible in Paris. Kiss the children for me, and present to Mme Stravinsky my respectful compliments. Believe in the affection of your devoted

MAURICE RAVEL

3

St. Jean de Luz
26th September 1914

Give me news of yourself, mon vieux. What becomes of you in all this?

Edouard[1] enlisted as a driver. I was not so lucky. They did not need me. I hope when they have re-examined all the discharged soldiers, and after all the measures I shall take, to be back in Paris, if I have the means.

The thought that I would go away forced me to do five months' work in five weeks. I have *finished* my Trio. But I was obliged to abandon the works I hoped to finish this winter; La Cloche Engloutie! ! and a symphonic poem: Wien! ! ![2] But, of course, that is now an untimely subject.

How is your wife? and the little ones? Write me quickly, mon vieux. If you only knew how painful it is to be far from everything!

Affectionate souvenirs to all. No news from the Benois. What has become of them?

MAURICE RAVEL

4

Paris, 14th November 1914

Cher vieux, I am back in Paris . . . and it does not suit me at

---

[1] His brother.
[2] Which became *La Valse*.

7. Drawing by Picasso, Rome, 1917

8. Drawing of Picasso by Stravinsky, 1920
'Tête de Picasso que je n'ai pas réussi(e)'

all. I want to go away more than ever. I cannot work any more. When we arrived Maman had to stay in bed. Now she is up, but she has to keep to an albumin-free diet. Her age and her anxieties are of course the cause of this condition. No news from Edouard since the 28th October; a whole month and we do not know what has happened to him.

Delage is now in Fontainebleau. From time to time he is sent on a commission somewhere. Schmitt,[1] who was bored to death in Toul, finally obtained permission to go to the front. The Godebskis[2] are still at Carantec. I still haven't seen Misia.

Remember me to your family, cher vieux. Write to me very soon I beg you. Believe in my brotherly friendship.

MAURICE RAVEL

5

19th December 1914

Vieux, it's settled: you come and sleep (uncomfortably) in the lumber room, which was the bedroom of my brother, and which was transformed into a Persian room for you. But come quickly, otherwise you will not find me here any more. I will be working as a driver. It was the only means for me to get to the city where I had to see *Daphnis et Chloe.* You don't give me news from your brother. I hope he is completely recovered. Try to hasten your arrival.

Our affectionate thoughts to you.
MAURICE RAVEL

6

2nd January 1915

Ainsi, vieux. Everything was prepared to give you, our ally,

[1] Florent Schmitt.

[2] Cipa Godebski, with his wife and children, Jean and Mimi. The Godebskis (especially Misia Godebski Sert) were good friends to Ravel and to me. The issue of *L'Oeil* for Christmas 1956 contains a history of this extraordinary family.

a proper welcome. The Persian room with voiles from Genoa, prints from Japan, toys from China, in short a synthesis of the 'Russian Season'. Yes, there was even a mechanical Nightingale—and you are not coming. . . . Ah, the caprice of the Slav! Is it thanks to this caprice that I received a note from Szántó[1] who is delighted to know that I will be in Switzerland at the end of January? I wrote you that I will soon be away, but I doubt that they will send me in your direction.

I wait for news from your brother and from you and all your family. Meanwhile, accept all our affectionate wishes for the New Year (New Style).

> Devotedly,
>
> MAURICE RAVEL

7

16th September 1919

Dear Igor,

I am heartbroken that I did not see you. Why didn't you phone Durand?[2] They would have given you my address and my telephone number (St. Cloud 2.33). Well, I hope to meet you soon, perhaps even in Morges because I will try to go there to see my uncle before the end of the fall. I continue to do nothing. I am probably empty. Give me your news soon and if you go through Paris again try to be a little bit cleverer and do a little better.

> To everybody my affectionate greetings,
>
> MAURICE RAVEL

---

[1] Pianist and composer, acquaintance of all of us, he made a piano transcription of the 'Chinese March' in my *Nightingale*.

[2] The publishers.

8

Dear Igor,

Your *Noces* are marvellous! And I regret that I couldn't hear and see more performances of them. But it seemed already unwise to come the other evening; my foot was again very swollen and I now have to go back and rest again until next Sunday at least. Thank you, mon vieux,

Affectionately,

MAURICE RAVEL

SATIE

R.C. What do you recall of Erik Satie?

I.S. He was certainly the oddest person I have ever known, but the most rare and consistently witty person, too. I had a great liking for him and he appreciated my friendliness, I think, and liked me in return. With his pince-nez, umbrella, and galoshes he looked a perfect schoolmaster, but he looked just as much like one without these accoutrements. He spoke very softly, hardly opening his mouth, but he delivered each word in an inimitable, precise way. His handwriting recalls his speech to me: it is exact, drawn. His manuscripts were like him also, which is to say as the French say '*fin*'. No one ever saw him wash—he had a horror of soap. Instead he was forever rubbing his fingers with pumice. He was always very poor, poor by conviction, I think. He lived in a poor section and his neighbours seemed to appreciate his coming among them: he was greatly respected by them. His apartment was also very poor. It did not have a bed but only a hammock. In winter Satie would fill bottles with hot water and put them flat in a row underneath his hammock. It looked like some strange kind of marimba. I remember once when someone had promised him some money he replied: 'Monsieur, what you have said did not fall on a deaf ear.'

His sarcasm depended on French classic usages. The first time I heard *Socrate*, at a séance where he played it for a few of us, he turned around at the end and said in perfect bourgeoisie: 'Voila, messieurs, dames.'

I met him in 1913, I believe, at any rate I photographed him with Debussy in that year. Debussy introduced him to me and Debussy 'protected' and remained a good friend to him. In those early years he played many of his compositions for me at the piano. (I don't think he knew much about instruments and I prefer *Socrate* as he played it to the clumsy orchestra score.) I always thought them literarily limited. The titles are literary, and whereas Klee's titles are literary they do not limit the painting; Satie's do, I think, and they are very much less amusing the second time. But the trouble with *Socrate* is that it is metrically boring. Who can stand that much regularity? All the same, the music of Socrates' death is touching and dignifying in a unique way. Satie's own sudden and mysterious death—shortly after *Socrate*—touched me too. He had been turned towards religion near the end of his life and he started going to Communion. I saw him after church one morning and he said in that extraordinary manner of his: 'Alors, j'ai un peu communiqué ce matin.' He became ill very suddenly and died quickly and quietly.

SCHOENBERG, BERG, WEBERN

R.C. Will you describe your meeting with Schoenberg in Berlin in 1912? Did you speak German with him? Was he cordial or aloof? Was he an able conductor of *Pierrot*? Webern was present at the Berlin rehearsals of *Pierrot*; do you have any recollection of him? You wrote about the instrumentation of *Pierrot* but not about its use of strict contrapuntal devices or its polyphony; how did you feel about these innovations at the time?

I.S. Diaghilev invited Schoenberg to hear my ballets, *Firebird* and *Petroushka*, and Schoenberg invited us to hear his *Pierrot lunaire*. I do not remember whether Schoenberg or Scherchen or Webern conducted the rehearsals I heard. Diaghilev and I spoke German with Schoenberg and he was friendly and warm and I had the feeling that he was interested in my music, especially in *Petroushka*. It is difficult to recollect one's impressions at a distance of forty-five years; but this I remember very clearly: the instrumental substance of *Pierrot Lunaire* impressed me immensely. And by saying 'instrumental' I mean not simply the instrumentation of this music but the whole contrapuntal and polyphonic structure of this brilliant instrumental masterpiece. Unfortunately I do not remember Webern—though I am sure I did at least meet him, in Schoenberg's house in Zehlendorf. Immediately after the war I received some very cordial letters from Schoenberg inquiring about various small pieces of mine that he and Webern were preparing for performance in his famous Vienna concert series, the Society for Private Performances. Then in 1925, he wrote a very nasty verse about me (though I almost forgive him, for setting it to such a remarkable mirror canon). I do not know what had happened in between.

R.C. And Berg, did you know him?

I.S. I met him only once, in Venice, in September 1934. He came to see me in the green room at La Fenice, where I conducted my *Capriccio* in a Biennale concert with my son, Soulima, at the piano. Although it was my first sight of him and I saw him for only a few minutes, I remember I was quite taken by his famous charm and subtlety.

R.C. Has your estimate of Schoenberg and his position been

affected by the recent publication of his unfinished works?

I.S.   His scope is greatly enlarged by them, but I think his position remains the same. However, any newly revealed work by a master will challenge judgment of him in some particular—as Eliot says that Dante's minor works are of interest because they are by Dante, so anything by Schoenberg, a piece of incunabula like the 1897 string Quartet, an arrangement like his 1900 reduction for two pianos of the *Barber of Seville*, is of interest to us because it is by Schoenberg. The most interesting of the unfinished works are the three pieces for an ensemble of solo instruments composed in 1910. They force us to reconsider the extent of Webern's indebtedness respecting instrumental style and the dimension of the short piece.[1] The last composed of the unfinished works, the *Modern Psalms* of 1950-1 show that Schoenberg continued to explore new ways and to search for new laws of serial music right up to his death. Of these posthumous publications *Moses und Aron* is in a category by itself: whereas the other works are unfinished, it is unfinished but complete—like Kafka stories in which the nature of the subject makes an ending in the ordinary sense impossible. *Moses und Aron* is the largest work of Schoenberg's maturity and the last he was to write in Europe. It does not affect our view of his historical role, however. *Jacob's Ladder*, or the hundred bars of it that are in a performable state might still do that:[2] it dates from Schoenberg's period of greatest transition, is actually the only composition to represent the years 1915-22. Schoenberg's work has too many inequalities for us to embrace it as a

[1] No. I have heard these pieces several times since. They are not much like Webern, and the most memorable of them, the third one, is very unlike Webern indeed.

[2] I now find *Jacob's Ladder* disappointing, and its *Sprechstimme* choruses less good than the beginning of *Die glückliche Hand*. The latter work is, in fact, so striking that it robs not only *Jacob's Ladder* but even a work like Boulez's *Le Visage Nuptial* of originality.

whole. For example, nearly all of his texts are appallingly bad, some of them so bad as to discourage performance of the music. Then too, his orchestrations of Bach, Handel, Monn, Loewe, Brahms differ from the type of commercial orchestration only in the superiority of craftsmanship: his intentions are no better. Indeed, it is evident from his Handel arrangement that he was unable to appreciate music of 'limited' harmonic range, and I have been told that he considered the English virginalists, and in fact any music that did not show a 'developing harmony', primitive. His expressionism is of the naïvest sort, as, for example, in the directions for lighting the *Glückliche Hand*; his late tonal works are as dull as the Reger they resemble, or the César Franck, for the four-note motive in the *Ode to Napoleon* is like César Franck; and, his distinction between 'inspired melody' and mere 'technique' ('heart' *v.* 'brain') would be factitious if it weren't simply naïve, while the example he offers of the former, the unison *Adagio* in his fourth Quartet makes me squirm. We—and I mean the generation who are now saying 'Webern and me'—must remember only the perfect works, the *Five Pieces for Orchestra* (except for which I could bear the loss of the first nineteen opus numbers), *Herzgewächse*, *Pierrot*, the *Serenade*, the *Variations* for orchestra, and, for its orchestra, the *Seraphita* song from op. 22. By these works Schoenberg is among the great composers. Musicians will take their bearings from them for a great while to come. They constitute together with a few works of not so many other composers, the true tradition.

R.C. How do you now esteem Berg's music?

I.S. If I were able to penetrate the barrier of style (Berg's radically alien emotional climate) I suspect he would appear to me as the most gifted constructor in form of the composers of this century. He transcends even his own most overt modelling. In fact, he is the only one to have achieved large-scale development-type forms without a suggestion of 'neo-classic' dissimulation. His legacy contains very little on which to build, however. He is at the end of a development (and form and style are not such independent growths that we can pretend to use the one and discard the other) whereas Webern, the Sphinx, has bequeathed a whole foundation, as well as a contemporary sensibility and style. Berg's forms are thematic (in which respect, as in most others, he is Webern's opposite); the essence of his work is thematic structure, and the thematic structure is responsible for the immediacy of the form. However complex, however 'mathematical' the latter are, they are always 'free' thematic forms born of 'pure feeling' and 'expression'. The perfect work in which to study this, and, I think, the essential work, with *Wozzeck*, for the study of all of his music, is the *Three Pieces for Orchestra*, op. 6. Berg's personality is mature in these pieces, and they seem to me a richer and freer expression of his talent than the twelve-note serial pieces. When one considers their early date—1914, Berg was twenty-nine—they are something of a miracle. I wonder how many musicians have discovered them even now, forty years later. In many places they suggest the later Berg. The music at bar 54 in *Reigen* is very like the 'death' motive first heard in Marie's aria in *Wozzeck* for example. So is the drowning music in the opera like the music from bar 162 in the *Marsch*. The waltz and the music at bar 50 in *Reigen*, is Wozzeckian in the manner of the second act's Tavern Scene, and the trill music with which *Reigen* ends is like the famous orchestra trill at the end of the first act of *Wozzeck*. The violin solo at bar 168 in the *Marsch* is an adumbration of the music of the last pages of *Wozzeck*, and the rhythmic polyphony of the motive at bar 75 in the same piece is like a quotation from the opera. There are forecasts of the *Kammerkonzert*, too, for instance, in the *Nebenstimme* figure at bar 55 in *Reigen* and in the solo violin and wind music thereafter. And, each of *Lulu*'s three acts concludes with the same rhythm of chords employed near the end of *Reigen.*

Mahler dominates rather too much of the *Marsch* but even that piece is saved by a superb (un-Mahler-like) ending, that is—I hope I may be forgiven for pointing out—dramatically not unlike the ending of *Petroushka*: climax followed by quiet, then a few broken phrases in solo instruments, then the final protest of trumpets; the last bar in the trumpets is one of the finest things Berg ever did. *The Three Pieces for Orches· tra* must be considered as a whole. They are a dramatic whole and all three of them are related thematically (the superb return of the theme of the *Preludium* at bar 160 in the *Marsch*). The form of each individual piece is dramatic also. In my judgment the most perfect of these in conception and realization is the *Preludium*. The form rises and falls, and it is round and unrepeating. It begins and ends in percussion, and the first notes of the timpani are already thematic. Then flute and bassoon state the principal rhythmic motive in preparation for the alto trombone solo, one of the noblest sounds Berg or anyone else ever caused to be heard in an orchestra. Berg's orchestral imagination and orchestral skill is phenomenal, especially in creating orchestral blocks, by which I mean balancing the whole orchestra in several polyphonic planes. One of the most remarkable noises he ever imagined is at bar 89 in *Reigen,* but there are many other striking sonorous inventions, the tuba entrance at bar 110 in *Reigen,* for instance, and bar 49 of the *Preludium,* and bar 144 of the *Marsch.*

I have a photograph on my wall of Berg and Webern together dating from about the time of the composition of the *Three Pieces for Orchestra.* Berg is tall, loose-set, almost too beautiful; his look is outward. Webern is short, hard-set, myopic, down-looking. Berg reveals an image of himself in his flowing 'artist's' cravat; Webern wears peasant-type shoes, and they are muddy—which to me reveals something profound. As I look at this photograph I cannot help remembering that so few years after it was taken both men died premature and tragic deaths after years of poverty, musical neglect, and, finally, musical banishment in their own country. I see Webern who in his last months frequented the churchyard at Mittersill where he was later buried, standing there in the quiet looking to the mountains—according to his daughter; and Berg in his last months suspecting that his illness might be fatal. I compare the fate of these men who heeded no claim of the world and who made music by which our half-century will be remembered, compare it with the 'careers' of conductors, pianists, violinists, vain excrescences all. Then this photograph of two great musicians, two pure-in-spirit, *herrliche Menschen*, restores my sense of justice at the deepest level.

*   *   *

R.C. Did you know Bartók personally?

I.S. I met him at least twice in my life, once in London, in the nineteen-twenties and later in New York in the early forties, but I had no opportunity to approach him closer either time. I knew the most important musician he was, I had heard wonders about the sensitivity of his ear, and I bowed deeply to his religiosity. However, I never could share his lifelong gusto for his native folklore. This devotion was certainly real and touching, but I couldn't help regretting it in the great musician. His death in circumstances of actual need has always impressed me as one of the tragedies of our society.

R.C. Do you still feel as you once did about the late Verdi (in the *Poetics of Music*)?

I.S. No. In fact, I am struck by the force, especially in *Falstaff*, with which he resisted Wagnerism, resisted or kept away from what had seized the advanced musical world. The presentation of musical monologues seems to me more original in *Falstaff* than in *Otello*. Original also are the instrumentation, harmony, and part-writing, yet none of these has left any element of the sort that could create a school—so different is

Verdi's originality from Wagner's. Verdi's gift is pure; but even more remarkable than the gift itself is the strength with which he developed it from *Rigoletto* to *Falstaff,* to name the two operas I love best.

R.C. Do you now admit any of the operas of Richard Strauss?

I.S. I would like to admit all Strauss operas to whichever purgatory punishes triumphant banality. Their musical substance is cheap and poor; it cannot interest a musician today. That now so ascendant *Ariadne*? I cannot bear Strauss's six-four chords: *Ariadne* makes me want to scream. Strauss himself? I had the opportunity to observe him closely during Diaghilev's production of his *Legend of Joseph,* more closely than at any other time. He conducted the *première* of that work and spent some time in Paris during the preparation. He never wanted to speak German with me, though my German was better than his French. He was very tall, bald, energetic, a picture of the *bourgeois allemand.* I watched him at rehearsals and I admired the way he conducted. His manner to the orchestra was not admirable, however, and the musicians heartily detested him; but every corrective remark he made was exact: his ears and his musicianship were impregnable. At that time his music reminded me of Böcklin and Stuck, and the other painters of what we then called the German Green Horrors. I am glad that young musicians today have come to appreciate the lyric gift in the songs of the composer Strauss despised, and who is more significant in our music than he is: Gustav Mahler. My low esteem for Strauss's operas is somewhat compensated by my admiration for von Hofmannsthal. I knew this fine poet and librettist well, saw him often in Paris, and, I believe, for the last time at the Berlin *première* of my *Oedipus Rex* (where Albert Einstein also came to greet me). Hofmannsthal was a man of enormous culture and very elegant charm. I have read him recently, last year before travelling to Hosios Loukas, his essay on that extraordinary place, and was pleased to think him still good. His *Notebooks* (1922) are one of my most treasured books.

R.C. Are you interested in the current revival of eighteenth-century Italian masters?

I.S. Not very. Vivaldi is greatly overrated—a dull fellow who could compose the same form so many times over. And, in spite of my predisposition in favour of Galuppi and Marcello (created more by Vernon Lee's *Studies of the Eighteenth Century in Italy* than by their music), they are poor composers. As for Cimarosa, I always expect him to abandon his four-times-four and turn into Mozart, and when he doesn't I am more exasperated than I should be if there had never been a Mozart. Caldara I respect largely because Mozart copied seven of his canons; I do not know much of his music. Pergolesi? *Pulcinella* is the only work of 'his' I like. Scarlatti is a different matter but even he varied the form so little. Living part of the last two years in Venice I have been exposed to an amount of this music. The Goldoni anniversary was an occasion to perform many Goldoni-libretto operas. I always regret I cannot fully appreciate Goldoni, with or without music—I do not understand his language—but Goldoni interests me more than his musicians. In the Teatro La Fenice or the Chiostro Verde of S. Giorgio, however, one likes everything a little bit more than one might elsewhere.

The 'Venetian' music I would like to revive is by Monteverdi and the Gabrielis, by Cipriano and Willaert, and so many others—why even the great Obrecht was 'Venetian' at one time—of that so much richer and so much closer-to-us period. True, I heard a Giovanni Gabrieli-Giovanni Croce concert there last year but almost nothing of the sense of their music remained. The tempi were wrong, the ornamentation didn't exist or was wrong when it did, the style and sentiment were ahead of the period by three and a half centuries, and the orchestra was eighteenth-century. When will musicians learn that the performance point of Gabrieli's music is rhythmic not harmonic? When will they stop trying to make mass choral effects out of simple harmonic changes and bring out, articulate, those marvellous rhythmic inventions? Gabrieli is rhythmic polyphony.

DYLAN THOMAS

R.C. What was the subject of the 'opera' you had planned to write with Dylan Thomas?

I.S. I don't think you can say that the project ever got as far as having a subject, but Dylan had a very beautiful idea.

I first heard of Dylan Thomas from Auden, in New York, in February or March of 1950. Coming late to an appointment one day Auden excused himself saying he had been busy helping to extricate an English poet from some sort of difficulty. He told me about Dylan Thomas. I read him after that, and in Urbana in the winter of 1950 my wife went to hear him read. Two years later, in January 1952, the English film producer, Michael Powell, came to see me in Hollywood with a project that I found very attractive. Powell proposed to make a short film, a kind of masque, of a scene from the Odyssey; it would require two or three arias as well as pieces of pure instrumental music and recitations of pure poetry. Powell said that Thomas had agreed to write the verse; he asked me to compose the music. Alas, there was no money. Where were the angels, even the Broadway kind, and why are the world's commissions, grants, funds, foundations never available to Dylan Thomases? I regret that this project was not realized. *The Doctor and the Devils* proves, I think, that Dylan's talent could have created the new medium.

Then in May 1953 Boston University proposed to commission me to write an opera with Dylan. I was in Boston at the time and Dylan who was in New York or New Haven came to see me. As soon as I saw him I knew that the only thing to do was to love him. He was nervous, however, chain smoking the whole time, and he complained of severe gout pains . . . 'but I prefer the gout to the cure; I'm not going to let a doctor shove a bayonet into me twice a week'.

His face and skin had the colour and swelling of too much drinking. He was a shorter man than I expected, from his portraits, not more than five feet five or six, with a large protuberant behind and belly. His nose was a red bulb and his eyes were glazed. He drank a glass of whisky with me which made him more at ease, though he kept worrying about his wife, saying he had to hurry home to Wales 'or it would be too late'. He talked to me about the *Rake's Progress.* He had heard the first broadcast of it from Venice. He knew the libretto well, and he admired it: 'Auden is the most skilful of us all.' I don't know how much he knew about music, but he talked about the operas he knew and liked, and about what he wanted to do. 'His' opera was to be about the rediscovery of our planet following an atomic misadventure. There would be a re-creation of language, only the new one would have no abstractions; there would be only people, objects, and words. He promised to avoid poetic indulgences: 'No conceits, I'll knock them all on the head.' He talked to me about Yeats who he said was almost the greatest lyric poet since Shakespeare, and quoted from memory the poem with the refrain 'Daybreak and a candle-end'. He agreed to come to me in Hollywood as soon as he could. Returning there I had a room built for him, an extension from our dining-room, as we have no guest room. I received two letters from him. I wrote him October 25th in New York and asked him for word of his arrival plans in Hollywood. I expected a telegram from him announcing the hour of his aeroplane. On November 9th the telegram came. It said he was dead. All I could do was cry.

About Musicians and Others

1

The Boat House, Laugharne,
Carmarthenshire, Wales.
16th June 1953

Dear Mr. Stravinsky,

I was so very glad to meet you for a little time, in Boston; and you and Mrs. Stravinsky couldn't have been kinder to me. I hope you get well very soon.

I haven't heard anything yet from Sarah Caldwell,[1] but I've been thinking a lot about the opera and have a number of ideas—good, bad, and chaotic. As soon as I can get something down on paper, I should, if I may, love to send it to you. I broke my arm just before leaving New York the week before last, and can't write properly yet. It was only a little break, they tell me, but it cracked like a gun.

I should very much like—if you think you would still like me to work with you; and I'd be enormously honoured and excited to do that—to come to California in late September or early October. Would that be convenient? I hope so. And by that time, I hope too, to have some clearer ideas about a libretto.

Thank you again. And please give my regards to your wife and to Mr. Craft.

Yours sincerely,

DYLAN THOMAS

2

The Boat House, Laugharne,
Carmarthenshire, Wales,
22nd September 1953

Dear Igor Stravinsky,

Thank you very very much for your two extremely nice letters, and for showing me the letter you had written to Mr.

[1] Of Boston University.

79

Choate of Boston University. I would have written again long before this, but I kept on waiting until I knew for certain when I would be able to come to the States; and the lecture agent there in New York, who makes my coming across possible, has been terribly slow in arranging things. I heard from him only this week. Now it is certain that I shall be in New York on the 16th of October; and I'll have to stay there, giving some poetry-readings and taking part in a couple of performances of a small play of mine, until the end of October. I should like then, if I may, to come straight to California to be with you and to get down together, to the first stage of our work. (I'm sure I needn't tell you how excited I am to be able to write down that word 'our'. It's wonderful to think of.)

One of my chief troubles is, of course, money. I haven't any of my own, and most of the little I make seems to go to schools for my children, who will persist in getting older all the time. The man who's arranged my readings in October, at a few Eastern Universities and at the Poetry Center, New York, is paying my expenses to and from New York. But from there to California I will have to pay my own way on what I can make out of these readings. I do hope it will work out all right. Maybe I'll be able to give a few other readings or rantings, in California to help pay expenses. (I'd relied on drawing my travelling expenses, etc., from the original Boston University Commission.) I want to bring my wife, Caitlin, with me, and she thinks she can stay with a friend in San Francisco while I am working with you in Hollywood. Anyway, I'll have to work these things out the best I can, and I mustn't bother you with them now. Money for California will come somehow, I'll pray for ravens to drop some in the desert. The *main* thing, I know, is for me to get to you as soon as possible, so that we can begin—well, so that we can *begin*, whatever it will turn out to be. I've been thinking an awful lot about it.

9. With Diaghilev at the Alfonso XIII Hotel, Seville, 1921

10. Venice, the Kings of the Tetrarch (Palazzo Ducale), 1925

About Musicians and Others

I was so sorry to hear that you had been laid up for so long; I hope you're really well again by this time. My arm's fine now and quite as weak as the other one.

If you don't write to me at Wales before I leave, about October 7th, then my American address will be: c/o J. M. Brinnin, Poetry Center, YM-YWHA, 1395 Lexington Avenue, New York, 28. But anyway I'll write again as soon as I reach there.

I'm looking forward enormously to meeting you again, and to working with you. And I *promise* not to tell anyone about it—(though it's very hard not to).

Most sincerely,

DYLAN THOMAS

3

ABOUT MY LIFE AND TIMES
AND OTHER ARTS

R.C. I once heard you describe your childhood glimpses of the
Tsar Alexander III.

I.S. I saw the Tsar many times while walking with my brothers
and governess along the quays of St. Petersburg's Moyka
River or by the adjacent canals. The Tsar was a very large
man. He occupied the entire seat of a droshky driven by a
troika coachman as big and obese as himself. The coachman
wore a dark blue uniform, the chest of which was covered
with medals. He was seated in front of the Tsar, but elevated
on the driver's seat where his enormous behind, like a gigan-
tic pumpkin, was only a few inches from the Tsar's face. The
Tsar had to answer greetings from people in the street by
raising his right hand towards his temple. As he was recognized by everybody he was obliged to do this almost without
interruption. His appearances gave me great pleasure and I
eagerly anticipated them. We removed our hats and received
the Tsar's acknowledging gesture, feeling very important
indeed.

I also saw the same Tsar in an unforgettable pageant, a
parade that passed our street on its way to the Imperial
Mariinsky Theatre. It honoured the Shah of Persia and was

the climax of an important state visit. We were given places in the first-floor window of our hairdresser's. The most brilliant procession of all kinds of cavalry passed by, imperial guards, coaches with grand dukes, ministers, generals. I remember a long, forest-like noise, the 'hurrah' of the crowds in the streets, coming in crescendo waves closer and closer with the approaching isolated car of the Tsar and the Shah.

R.C. Your father and Dostoievsky were friends. I suppose you as a child heard a great deal about Dostoievsky?

I.S. Dostoievsky became in my mind the symbol of the artist continually in need of money. My mother talked about him in this way; she said he was always grubbing. He gave readings from his own works and these were supported by my parents, who complained, however, that they were intolerably boring. Dostoievsky liked music and often went to concerts with my father.

Incidentally, I still consider Dostoievsky to be the greatest Russian after Pushkin. Now when one is supposed to reveal so much of oneself by one's choice of Freud or Jung, Stravinsky or Schoenberg, Dostoievsky or Tolstoy, I am a Dostoievskyan.

R.C. I have heard you say you saw Ibsen 'plain'.

I.S. In May 1905, shortly after the separation of Norway and Sweden, I and my younger brother, Goury, went on a holiday to Scandinavia where we stayed for about a month. We sailed from St. Petersburg to Kronstadt and Helsingfors, staying in the latter city for a few days with my uncle, who was the civil governor of Finland. We then sailed to Stockholm, stopping long enough to hear a performance of the *Marriage of Figaro*, and through the beautiful Swedish lake canals to Göteborg, where we changed boats for Copenhagen and Oslo. It was delicious spring weather in Oslo, cold but pleasant. One day it seemed as if the whole population was in the streets. We were riding in a droshky and the friend who was with us told me to look at a smallish man on the sidewalk to our right. It was Henrik Ibsen. He wore a top hat and his hair was white. He was walking with his hands folded behind his back. Some things one sees never leave the eyes, never move into the back part of the mind. So Ibsen is in my eyes.

R.C. You were a friend of d'Annunzio's at one time, weren't you.?

I.S. I saw rather a lot of him just before the 1914 war, but Diaghilev had known him before me; he was a great enthusiast of our Russian Ballet. I met him for the first time in Paris at Mme Golubev's, a Russian lady of the Mme Récamier school—throughout one's entire audience she would remain on a divan with her elbow raised and her head propped on her hand. One day, d'Annunzio entered her *salon*, a small man, brisk and natty, very perfumed and very bald (Harold Nicolson's likening his head to an egg, in *Some People*, is an exact comparison). He was a brilliant, fast, and very amusing talker, so unlike the 'talk' in his books. I remember that he was very excited about my opera *The Nightingale*; when after its *première* the French press had generally attacked it he wrote an article in its defence, an article I wish I still had. I saw him many times after that. He came to my apartment in Paris, he came to performances of the Ballet and to concerts of mine in France and Italy. Then, suddenly, it was discovered that his execrable taste in literature went together with Mussolini's execrable taste in everything else. He was no longer a 'character' and no longer amusing. But whether or not he survives as a readable author, his influence does still survive: the interiors of many Italian homes still follow descriptions in his novels.

On a recent visit to Asolo, to see the composer Malipiero, I was strongly reminded of d'Annunzio. Malipiero has a most extraordinary and not entirely un-d'Annunzian house, a fine Venetian building on a hillside. One enters under a Latin inscription and plunges into darkest night. The dark is in deference to pairs of owls who, from covered cages in obscure corners, hoot the two notes,

in tune with Malipiero's piano after he plays them. There is evidence in the garden of affection for other of God's feathered creatures: chickens have been buried in marked graves; Malipiero's chickens die of old age.

R.C. You knew Rodin, didn't you?

I.S. I made his acquaintance in the Grand Hotel in Rome shortly after the beginning of the First World War. Diaghilev had organized a benefit concert there in which I conducted the Suite from *Petroushka*. I confess I was more interested in him because of his fame than because of his art for I did not share the enthusiasm of his numerous and serious admirers. I met him again, some time later, at one of our ballet performances in Paris. He greeted me kindly, as though I were an old acquaintance, and at that moment I remembered the impression his fingers had made on me at our first handshaking. They were soft, quite the contrary of what I had expected, and they did not seem to belong to a male hand, especially not to a sculptor's hand. He had a long white beard that reached down to the navel of his long, buttoned-up surtout, and white hair covered his entire face. He sat reading a Ballet Russe programme through a pince-nez while people waited impatiently for the great old artist to stand up as they passed in his row—not knowing it was he. It has been said that Rodin drew a sketch of me. To the best of my knowledge that is not so. Perhaps the author of that information was confusing him with Bonnard who did in fact make a fine ink portrait of me in 1913—lost, unfortunately, with all of my belongings, in our estate in Russia.

R.C. Wasn't there also a question of Modigliani doing a portrait of you?

I.S. Yes. I don't remember the circumstances very clearly, but I visited him in company with Leon Bakst in 1912 or 1913 because either he or I or Diaghilev had conceived the project of his doing a portrait. I don't know why it wasn't realized, whether Modigliani was ill, as he so often was, or whether I was called away with the Ballet. At that time I had an immense admiration for him.[1]

R.C. One more 'painter' question. I once heard you describe your meeting Claude Monet.

I.S. I don't know where Diaghilev found the old man or how he managed to get him into a loge at one of our Ballet Russe spectacles, but I saw him there and came to *serrer la main*. It was after the war, in 1922 or 1923, I think, and of course no one would believe it *was* Claude Monet. He wore a white beard and was nearly blind. I know now what I wouldn't have believed then, that he was painting his greatest pictures at the time, those huge, almost abstract canvases of pure colour and light (ignored until recently; I believe they are in the Orangeries, but a very beautiful *Water Lilies*, which now looks as good as any art of the period, I go to see in the Museum of Modern Art every time I am in New York[2]). Old Monet, hoary and near blind couldn't have impressed me more if he had been Homer himself.

R.C. You were with Mayakovsky very often on his famous Paris trip in 1922?

[1] A portrait of me by Modigliani has been discovered since these remarks were written. It is a large picture in grey, black, and ivory oils, undated but similar in period style to the Max Jacob and Cocteau portraits. It has been certified by such experts as Zborovsky, Schoeller, and Georges Guillaume and by a statement from Picasso: 'Je pense que ce tableau est une portrait de Stravinsky. Cannes, le 18.9.57 (signé) Picasso.' Modigliani must have done it from memory. I regret to admit that it does resemble me.

[2] Alas, since I wrote this, the *Water Lilies* has been destroyed by fire.

I.S. Yes, but he was a closer friend to Prokofiev than to me. I remember him as a somewhat burly youth—he was twenty-eight or twenty-nine at the time—who drank more than he should have and who was deplorably dirty, like many of the poets I have known. Sometimes I am reminded of him when I see a photograph of Gromyko, though I don't know just where the resemblance is. I considered him a good poet and I admired and still do admire his verses. However, he insisted on talking to me about music, and his understanding of that art was wholly imaginary. He spoke no French, and therefore with him I was always obliged to be a translator. I remember one such occasion when I was between him and Cocteau. Curiously, I found the French for everything Mayakovsky said very easily, but not the Russian for Cocteau's remarks. His suicide a few years later was the first of the shocks that were to come regularly from Russia thereafter.

R.C. Raymond Radiguet was often in your company the year before his death. How do you remember him?

I.S. I saw him almost every day of 1922 that I spent in Paris. He was a silent youth with a serene, rather childlike look, but with something of the young bull in him, too. He was of medium build, handsome, rather pederastically so but without pederastic manners. The first time I saw him he was with Cocteau. I was sitting with Diaghilev in a café when they appeared.

S.D.: 'Qu'est ce que c'est, ce nouveau truc?'

I.S.: 'Tu l'envies?'

He immediately struck me as a gifted individual and he also had the other intelligence, the *machine à penser* kind. His opinions were immediate and they were his, whereas the opinions of those around him were too often 'composed'. I still think his poems very good indeed, and the two novels hardly less good. The latter were autobiographical, of course, and everyone in Paris knew who was who. But I remember that when Radiguet died (at twenty) even the man effigied as the Comte d'Orgel in the book was greatly grieved.

R.C. While you are reminiscing, would you describe your last meeting with Proust?

I.S. After the *premières* of *Mavra* and *Renard* in June 1922, I went to a party given by a friend of mine, Princess Violette Murat. Marcel Proust was there also. Most of the people came to that party from my *première* at the Grand Opera, but Proust came directly from his bed, getting up as usual very late in the evening. He was a pale man, elegantly and Frenchly dressed, wearing gloves and carrying a cane. I talked to him about music and he expressed much enthusiasm for the late Beethoven quartets—enthusiasm I would have shared were it not a commonplace among the intellectuals of that time and not a musical judgment but a literary pose.

R.C. Klee, Kandinsky, and Busoni attended the 1923 Weimar performance of *L'Histoire du Soldat*. Do you remember anything about these gentlemen at the time?

I.S. I was only a very short time at Weimar—just long enough for the rehearsals and the performance of *L'Histoire*, conducted by Hermann Scherchen. Of the three artists you mention, I met only Ferruccio Busoni, who was sitting at this performance in the same box as I was. He had the noblest, most beautiful head I have ever seen and I watched him as much as the stage. He seemed to be very much touched by the work. But whether it was the play of Ramuz, my music, or the whole thing, was not easy to determine, especially since I knew that I was his *bête noire* in music. Now, thirty-five years later, I have a great admiration for his vision, for his literary talent, and for at least one of his works, *Doktor Faust*. Unfortunately, I did not meet Paul Klee there or later in my life.[1] I did have the good fortune to know Kandinsky in Paris in the nineteen-thirties, and I will always remember him as an aristocrat, *un homme de choix*.

[1] Klee's portrait drawing of me must have been done from memory.

R.C. I often hear you speak of your admiration for Ortega y Gasset. Did you know him well?

I.S. I saw him only once, in Madrid, in March 1955, but I felt I knew him from his work long before that. That night in Madrid he came to my hotel with Mme La Marquise de Slauzol, and we drank a bottle of whisky together and were very gay. He was charming and very kind. I have often thought since that he must have been aware that he had cancer; a few months later he was dead. He was not tall, but I remember him as a large man because of his great head. His bust reminded me of a Roman statesman or philosopher and I tried all evening to recall just which Roman he really was. He spoke vivid r-rolling French in a strong, slightly husky voice. Everything he said was vivid. The Tagus at Toledo was 'arteriosclerotic'; Cordoba was 'a rose bush but with the flowers in the ground and the roots in the air'. The art of the Portuguese 'is their memory of China, of pagodas'. Of his philosopher contemporaries, he spoke reverently of Scheler, of Husserl, of his master Cohen, of Heidegger. As for the Wittgenstein school: 'Philosophy calling itself Logical Positivism now claims to be a science, but this is only a brief attack of modesty.' He talked about Spain (I regret his *Castles in Castile* does not exist in English) and laughed at tourists' sentiments 'for the poor people living in caves' which he said they do not do out of poverty but because it is a very ancient tradition. He was sympathetic and intelligent about the United States when we talked of them—the unique European 'intellectual' I encountered that trip who knew something about them beyond what he had read in Melville and the magazines. He proudly showed me a photograph, which he took from his wallet, of himself and Gary Cooper taken in Aspen in 1949. He said that Thornton Wilder had translated for him there but that his audiences had understood before the translations came, 'because of my extravagant gestures'.

R.C. How did Giacometti come to make his drawings of you?

I.S. He had done five or six designs from photographs before he saw me, and he didn't like them. Then, sitting a few feet from me, he did a whole series, working very fast with only a few minutes of actual drawing for each one. He says that in sculpture also he accomplishes the final product very quickly, but does the sometimes hundreds of discarded preparatory ones slowly over long periods of time. He drew with a very hard lead, smudging the lines with erasers from time to time. He was forever mumbling: 'Non . . . impossible . . . je ne peux pas . . . une tête violente . . . je n'ai pas de talent . . . je ne peux pas. . . .' He surprised me the first time he came for I expected a 'Giacometti' tall and thin. He said he had just escaped from an automobile manufacturer who had been offering him a considerable sum to say that automobiles and sculptures are the same things, i.e., beautiful objects. In fact, Giacometti's almost favourite topic was the difference between a sculpture and an object. 'Men in the street walking in different directions are not objects in space.' 'Sculpture,' he said, 'is a *matière* transformed into expression, expression in which nature counts for less than style.' 'Sculpture is expression in space, which means that it can never be complete; to be complete is to be static.' 'All busts are ridiculous; the whole body is the only subject for sculpture.'

His conversation about sculptors was sometimes surprising. He liked Pigalle, thought him the greatest sculptor of the *dix-huitième*, especially in the memorial of the Maréchal de Saxe at Strasbourg. He much preferred Pigalle's rejected 'nude Voltaire' to Houdon's famous official Voltaire 'because of its greater nervousness'. For him Canova was not really a sculptor, while Rodin was 'the last great sculptor and in the same line as Donatello (not the Rodin of the Balzac or the Burghers, of course)'. Brancusi wasn't a sculptor at all, he said, but a 'maker of objects'. I like Giacometti's work—I have one of those full-of-sculptural-space paintings of his on my dining-room wall—and I have an affection for himself, for his own 'nervousness'. I like the character of him in a story he told me. He had a great admiration for Klee and one time in the late nineteen-thirties, when both artists were living in Switzerland, he at last determined to go and call on him. He walked from the station to what he thought was Klee's house—it was on a mountain-side some distance from the town—but when he arrived there he discovered that Klee actually lived farther up on the mountain. 'I lost all courage and didn't go—I had just enough courage to get that far.'

PAINTERS OF THE RUSSIAN BALLET

R.C. Do you remember Balla's set for your *Fireworks*?

I.S. Vaguely, but I couldn't have described it even at the time (Rome, 1917) as anything more than a few splashes of paint on an otherwise empty backcloth. I do remember that it baffled the audience, however, and that when Balla came out to bow there was no applause: the public didn't know who he was, what he had done, why he should be bowing. Balla then reached in his pocket and squeezed a device that made his papillon necktie do tricks. This sent Diaghilev and me—we were in a box—into uncontrollable laughter, but the audience remained dumb.

Balla was always amusing and always likeable and some of the drollest hours of my life were spent in his and his fellow Futurists' company. The idea of doing a Futurist ballet was Diaghilev's but we decided together on my *Fireworks* music: it was 'Modern' enough and only four minutes long. Balla had impressed us as a gifted painter and we asked him to design a set. I made fast friends with him after that, visiting him often in his apartment in Rome. He lived near the zoo, so near in fact that his balcony overhung a large cage. One heard animal noises in his rooms as one hears street noises in a New York hotel room.

Futurism's headquarters were in Milan, however, and it was there that my meetings with Balla, and also Boccioni, Russolo the noise-maker, Carra and Marinetti took place. Milan was to Switzerland as Hollywood is to these hills except that it was easier then to take the train and descend to the Italian city for an evening performance than it is now to drive to downtown Los Angeles. And in wartime Milan my few Swiss francs made me feel agreeably rich.

On one of my Milanese visits Marinetti and Russolo, a genial, quiet man but with wild hair and beard, and Pratella, another noisemaker, put me through a demonstration of their 'Futurist Music'. Five phonographs standing on five tables in a large and otherwise empty room emitted digestive noises, static, etc., remarkably like the *musique concrète* of seven or eight years ago (so perhaps they were futurist after all; or perhaps Futurisms aren't progressive enough). I pretended to be enthusiastic and told them that sets of five phonographs with such music, mass produced, would surely sell like Steinway Grand Pianos.

Some years after this demonstration Marinetti invented what he called 'discreet noises', noises to be associated with objects. I remember one such sound (to be truthful, it wasn't at all discreet) and the object it accompanied, a substance that looked like velvet but had the roughest surface I have ever touched. Balla must have participated in the 'noise' movement, too, for he once gave me an Easter present, a *papier-mâché* Pascha cake that sighed very peculiarly when opened.

The most memorable event in all my years of friendship with the Futurists was a performance we saw together at the Milan puppet theatre of *The Chinese Pirates,* a 'drama in three acts'. It was in fact one of the most impressive theatrical experiences of my life. The theatre itself was puppet-sized. An invisible orchestra, clarinet, piano, violin, bass, played an overture and bits of incidental music. There were tiny windows on either side of the tiny stage. In the last act we heard singing and were terrified to see that it came from giants standing behind these windows; they were normal-statured human singers, of course, but we were accustomed to the puppet scale.

The Futurists were absurd, but sympathetically so, and they were infinitely less pretentious than some of the later movements that borrowed from them—than Surrealism, for instance, which had more substance; unlike the Surrealists they were able to laugh at their own pose of artist-contra-Gentiles. Marinetti himself was a balalaika—a chatterbox—but he was also the kindest of men. I regret that he seemed to me the least gifted of the whole group—compared to Boccioni, Balla and Carra, who were all able painters. The Futurists were not the aeroplanes they wanted to be but they were at any rate a pack of very nice, noisy Vespas.

R.C. Did you choose Nicolas Roerich to do the *Sacre du Printemps* décors?

I.S. Yes. I had admired his sets for *Prince Igor* and imagined he might do something similar for the *Sacre*; above all, I knew he would not overload. Diaghilev agreed with me and accordingly, in the summer of 1912, I met Roerich in Smolensk and worked with him there in the country house of the Princess Tenischev, a patroness and liberal who had helped Diaghilev.

I still have a good opinion of Roerich's *Le Sacre*. He had designed a backdrop of steppes and sky, the *Hic Sunt Leones* country of old mapmakers' imaginations. The row of twelve blonde, square-shouldered girls against this landscape made a very striking tableau. And Roerich's costumes were said to have been historically exact as well as scenically satisfying.

I met Roerich, a blond-bearded, Kalmuck-eyed, pug-nosed

94

man, in 1904. His wife was a relative of Mitusov's, my friend and co-librettist of the *Nightingale*, and I often saw the Roerichs at Mitusov's St. Petersburg house. Roerich claimed descent from Rurik, the Russo-Scandinavian Ur-Prince. Whether or not this was true (he looked Scandinavian, but one can't say such things any more), he was certainly a *seigneur*. I became quite fond of him in those early years, though not of his painting, which was a kind of advanced Puvis de Chavannes. I was not surprised during the last war to hear of his secret activities and of his curious connection with Vice-President Wallace in Tibet; he looked as though he ought to have been either a mystic or a spy. Roerich came to Paris for *Le Sacre*, but he received very little attention and, after the *première*, disappeared, slighted I think, back to Russia. I never saw him again.

R.C. Was Henri Matisse your choice of painter for the *Chant du Rossignol* sets?

I.S. No, his collaboration was Diaghilev's idea entirely. In fact, I opposed it, but too directly (Amiel says: 'Every direct resistance ends in disaster'). The production, and especially Matisse's part in it, were failures. Diaghilev hoped Matisse would do something very Chinese and charming. All he did do, however, was to copy the China of the shops in the rue de la Boëtie. Matisse designed not merely the sets, as you say, but also the costumes and curtain.

Matisse's art has never attracted me, but at the time of the *Chant du Rossignol* I saw him often and liked him personally. I remember an afternoon together with him in the Louvre. He was never a rousing conversationalist, but he stopped in front of a Rembrandt and started to talk excitedly about it. At one point he took a white handkerchief from his pocket: 'Which is white, this handkerchief or the white in that picture? Even the absence of colour does not exist, but only "white" or each and every white.'

Our Matisse collaboration made Picasso very angry: 'Matisse! What is a Matisse? A balcony with a big red flower-pot falling all over it.'

R.C. Do you remember Golovine's décors for the first *Firebird*?

I.S. All I remember about them is that the costumes pleased me at the time. The curtain was the curtain of the Opéra. I do not remember how many sets Golovine did, but I am certain that if I were transported back to that *Firebird* of 1910 I would find them very opulent indeed.

Golovine was several years my senior, and he was not our first choice. Diaghilev wanted Vroubel, the most talented of all the Russian painters of that epoch, but Vroubel was dying or going mad. We also considered Benois but Diaghilev preferred Golovine for his realization of the fantastic scenes in *Russlan*; and Golovine's orientalism conformed to the ideals of Diaghilev's own magazine, *Mir Isskustva*, rather than to the academic orientalism then so popular. As an easel painter Golovine was a kind of Russian pointillist.

I do not remember Golovine at the first *Firebird* performance. Diaghilev probably did not have money enough to pay his trip (I myself received 1,000 roubles, £100, for the commission and the expenses of all the travel and stay in Paris). The first *Firebird*! I stood in the dark of the Opéra through eight orchestra rehearsals conducted by Pierné. The stage and the whole theatre glittered at the *première* and that is all I remember.

R.C. How do you regard Leon Bakst?

I.S. No one could describe him as concisely as Cocteau has done in his caricature. We were friends from our first meeting in St. Petersburg, in 1909, though our conversation was largely Bakst's accounts of his exploits in the conquest of women, and my incredulity: 'Now Lev . . . you couldn't have done all that.' Bakst wore elegant hats, canes, spats, etc., but I think these were meant to detract from his Venetian comedy-mask

11. New York, 1954, listening to recording playbacks

12. Listening to a rehearsal of the *Canticum Sacrum* conducted by
Robert Craft in San Marco, Venice, September, 1956
(*Columbia Records Photograph*)

nose. Like other dandies, Bakst was sensitive—and privately mysterious. Roerich told me that 'Bakst' was a Jewish word meaning 'little umbrella'. Roerich said he discovered this one day in Minsk, when he was caught in a thunder-shower and heard people sending their children home for 'Baksts', which then turned out to be what he said they were.

There was a question of Bakst designing *Mavra* for me, but a money quarrel resulted with Diaghilev. None of us was ever reconciled and I regretted it, especially when only three years later, aboard the *Paris* on my first trip to the United States, I saw the notice of his death in the ship's newspaper.

Bakst loved Greece and all things Greek. He travelled there with Serov (Serov was the conscience of our whole circle and a very important friend to me in my youth; even Diaghilev feared him) and published a book of travel diaries called *With Serov in Greece* (1922) that ought to have been put into English long ago.

I had seen Bakst's easel painting before I knew any of his theatrical work, but I could not admire it. In fact, it represented everything in Russia against which *Le Sacre du Printemps* is the revolt. I consider Bakst's *Sheherazade* to be a masterpiece, however, perhaps the perfect achievement of the Russian Ballet from the scenic point of view. Costumes, sets, the curtain, were colourful in an indescribable way—we are so much poorer in these things now. I remember, too, that Picasso considered *Sheherazade* a masterpiece. In fact, it was the one production of the ballet he really did admire: 'Vous savez, c'est très spécialiste, mais admirablement fait.'

R.C. And Benois?

I.S. I knew him before I knew Bakst. He was at that time the most cultivated Italophile I had ever met, and except for Eugene Berman he would be still: and Benois and Berman are very like in the fact of their Russian background, their Romantic theatre, their Italophilia. Benois knew more about music than any of the other painters, though of course the music he knew was nineteenth-century Italian opera. I think he liked my *Petroushka*, however, or at any rate, he wasn't calling it *Petroushka-ka* as many others of his generation were. But Benois was the conservative of the company and *Petroushka* was his exceptional work.

I collaborated with him in a small way before *Petroushka* with two orchestrations contributed to *Les Sylphides* (I doubt if I would like these arrangements today—I no longer care for that 'clarinet solo' kind of music). But though I was delighted with his work in *Les Sylphides* I wouldn't have chosen him to do *Petroushka* on the strength of it. My real friendship with him began in Rome in 1911 when I was finishing *Petroushka*. We stayed in the Albergo Italia near the Quattro Fontane and for two months were with each other every day.

Benois was very quickly up on his *amour propre*. The ballet's greatest success at that time was the *Spectre de la Rose* with Nijinsky, and Benois was plainly jealous of Bakst's role in that success. Jealousy accounts for an incident that occurred the following year. Benois was painting the backdrop of Petroushka's cell when Bakst happened on the set, picked up a brush, and started to help. Benois fairly flew at him.

R.C. And was Michel Larionov your choice of painter for *Renard*?

I.S. Diaghilev suggested him first, but he became my choice also. As you know, I composed *Renard* for the Princess Edmonde de Polignac. In 1914 I was cut off from my Russian estate money and lived in Switzerland on a very small income. Diaghilev could pay me nothing in those war years so I accepted a commission of 2,500 Swiss francs from the Princess de Polignac. Diaghilev was furious with jealousy (but Diaghilev was always jealous; I think I am fair in saying that about him and I certainly knew him well enough to be able to say it now). For two years he would not mention *Renard* to me (which didn't prevent him from talking about it to others:

'Our Igor, always money, money, money, and for what? This *Renard* is some old scraps he found in his dresser drawer').

Diaghilev visited me in Ouchy in January or February 1917 and I played *Les Noces* for him. He wept (it was very surprising to see this huge man weep), saying it had touched him more than anything he had ever heard, but he would not inquire about *Renard*, even though he knew I had completed it. And he knew also that the Princess Polignac had no theatre, that she had commissioned me only to help me, that she would give *Renard* to him to perform. (Some years later the Princess de Polignac gave an *avant-propos* piano performance of *Oedipus Rex* at her house and paid me 12,000 francs which I gave to Diaghilev to help finance the public performance.)

Larionov was a huge blond mujik of a man, even bigger than Diaghilev (Larionov, who had an uncontrollable temper, once knocked Diaghilev down). He made a vocation of laziness, like Oblomov, and we always believed that his wife, Goncharova, did his work for him. He was a talented painter, nevertheless, and I still like his *Renard* set and costumes. *Renard* was performed together with *Mavra*, as you know, and both works were preceded by a big orchestral ballet which made my small-scale pieces seem even smaller.

Renard was no huge success, but compared to it *Mavra* was even less of a 'hit'. *Mavra* was very ably designed by Survage, an unknown artist who had been commissioned after Diaghilev had quarrelled with Bakst. The *Mavra* failure annoyed Diaghilev. He was anxious to impress Otto Kahn, who attended the *première* in Diaghilev's box and who was to have brought the company to America. Otto Kahn's only comment was: 'I liked it all, then "poop" it ends too quickly.' Diaghilev asked me to change the ending. I refused, of course, and he never forgave me.

Another 'ballet' painter I saw a lot of at this time was Derain. I liked his *parigot* talk, liked him more than his pictures, in fact, though there are charming small Derains. He was a man of large build—Balthus's portrait of him is a good resemblance—and a copious drinker. During the latter activity furniture was sometimes smashed, but I always found Derain very agreeable. I mediated for him in a quarrel with Diaghilev, who wanted to change something in *La Boutique Fantasque*. In his later years Derain was a solitary figure and we no longer saw him at concerts or spectacles. My last meeting with him was an extraordinary coincidence. I was driving near Toulon and stopped to walk in a pine wood. I came upon someone standing before an easel, painting, and it turned out to be Derain.

* * *

Now that I have mentioned Derain I would also like to record my associations with some other artists, most of them associated with Diaghilev or the Ballet. I think, for example, of Alexis Jawlensky. Diaghilev had described him to me in St. Petersburg days as a strong follower of the new Munich school. In spite of this he was a contributor to *Mir Isskustva*; I say 'in spite' because Diaghilev considered the Munich school to be the ultimate in 'Boche' bad taste. I did not meet Jawlensky in Russia but in Switzerland. At the beginning of the war I was living in Morges and he in St. Prex, which is nearby. I sometimes walked with my children from our Morges house to his in St. Prex. He was always hospitable, and his studio was a little island of Russian colour that delighted my children.

Max Liebermann was another friend, especially during the first period of our Ballet in Berlin. I made his acquaintance, together with Gerhardt Hauptmann's, after a performance of *Petroushka* and I saw him quite often thereafter. He was a celebrated wit. In a story then circulating, a portrait painter commissioned to do von Hindenburg complains to Liebermann of his inability to draw von Hindenburg's features, whereupon Liebermann exclaims: 'Ich kann den Alten in den Schnee pissen.' As you know, it was Liebermann who nominated me to the Prussian Academy.

Jacques-Emile Blanche was another friend of my early Diaghilev years. He painted two portraits of me that are now in the Luxembourg. I remember sitting for him, and how he drew my head and features only after a great amount of modelling, while everything else, the body and the background, was added *in absentia*. This meant that one's legs might turn out too long and one's middle too capacious, or that one might find oneself promenading on the beach at Deauville, as I am made to do in one of my portraits. However, Blanche's faces were usually accurately characterized and that was the important thing. Blanche was a *fine mouche* for celebrities; he came to make my portrait almost the morning after the *première* of the *Firebird*.

Robert Delauney was another painter I saw very often at one time. He talked too much and too enthusiastically about 'modern art', but was otherwise quite likeable. He did a portrait of me too. I don't know what has become of it but it was certainly better than Albert Gleizes's cubist one, which is my moustache plus what-have-you. Delauney never did design a ballet for Diaghilev but he was often with him, and in Madrid, in 1921, we were all three constantly together.

Fernand Léger I knew throughout the Diaghilev period, but we were closer friends in the United States during the second war. I remember a French dinner we had prepared for him in our house in Hollywood in the dark early days of the war. It concluded with French Caporal cigarettes and Léger was so touched upon seeing these, he burst out crying. The Léger drawing of a parrot on our living-room wall was given to us by him at this time.

Pavel Tchelichev I met in 1922 in Berlin where I was awaiting my mother's arrival from the Soviet Union (she had been petitioning since the Revolution for permission to emigrate, had at last obtained it, but her boat was several times delayed). Tchelichev was talented and handsome and he was quick to understand the value of that combination in the Diaghilev *ambience*. I was not attracted by his earliest 'Russian style' paintings but his sets for Nabokov's ballet *Ode* convinced me of his abilities. Later he made my *Balustrade* one of the most visually satisfying of all my ballets.

Marc Chagall I had heard of in Diaghilev days from Larionov who belonged to Chagall's circle of Russian painters, but I first met him in New York. My wife, Vera de Bosset, had arranged with him for a show of his *Aleko* designs and sketches in her Hollywood gallery, *La Boutique*. Accordingly, we called on him one day in his Riverside Drive apartment. He was in mourning for his wife and he hardly spoke without mentioning her. (I now remember that Lipnitsky the photographer was there and made several photographs of us together, but I have never seen them.) Two or three years later Chagall was asked to do stage settings and costumes for my *Renard*. I regret very much that he refused (saying, as I was told, that he wanted to do only 'a major work of Stravinsky's'). I still hope he will one day do *Renard* and *Les Noces*; no one could be more perfect for them. Chagall's *Firebird* was a very flamboyant exhibition, though perhaps more successful in the painting than in the costumes. He made an ink portrait of me and presented it to me as a memento of our collaboration.

There were others too, like Marie Laurencin (though I couldn't like her *couleur de rose* painting; I like *rose*, of course, but not when I am *emmerdé* with it; and I had the same trouble with her *gris* after Cocteau said: 'Marie, tu as inventé les nuances de gris'); Constantine Brancusi; Braque (who gave valuable advice to my painter son, Theodore); André Bauchant (a kind man; the idea that he should decorate my

Apollo was entirely Diaghilev's, however, and his set for that ballet was very far from what I had in mind); Christian Bérard; and Georges Rouault (with whom my wife, Vera de Bosset, worked designing the ballet *Fils Prodigue*).

R.C. You must have seen a great deal of José Maria Sert in the Diaghilev days.

I.S. Yes, but his wife Misia was much more a friend to me and, in truth, I could not help finding Sert slightly ridiculous. The Serts were among the first people I met in Paris when I arrived there in 1910 (though they were not yet legally 'Serts'). He knew a great lot of 'interesting people', especially 'interesting *rich* people', and he was very good at getting commissions from them. I believe that he became a 'painter of the Russian Ballet' chiefly because he knew Fürstner, Richard Strauss's publisher. Diaghilev wanted Strauss to compose a ballet, and the only way he could get at him was through Fürstner. Sert became the ambassador of the project and therefore its painter. The ballet was the *Legend of Joseph*, as you know. Sert's sets for it were overcrowded and the result was not one of Diaghilev's greatest successes.

Sert might have figured more permanently in the history of painting as a subject. A big, black-bearded man, *démodé*-distinguished, he would have made an excellent portrait subject for Manet. His manner was very grand and he played at being Spanish, but he had a sense of humour that somewhat redeemed these affectations. I remember asking him once how he intended to move one of his huge murals, and his answer: 'You turn a little valve and it deflates to one-hundredth the size.' We came to the U.S. on the *Normandie* together in the nineteen-thirties and the last time I saw him was in the U.S. Poor Sert, he wanted to be a painter but his painting, alas, is *quelconque*.

R.C. Have you any notion where Picasso's backdrop for *Pulcinella* might be?

I.S.   It was in the dome of the Paris Opéra when I last heard, and completely faded save for the moon, whose yellow had been renewed, in part, by a cat. Diaghilev, I suppose, was in debt to the Director of the Opéra, and when our company withdrew after the *Pulcinella* performances the Picasso was kept there.

I have a vague recollection of meeting Picasso with Vollard at my friend Prince Argutinsky's about 1910, but I did not know him until 1917, when we were together in Rome. I immediately liked his flat, unenthusiastic manner of speaking, and his Spanish way of accenting each syllable; 'He ne suis pas musicien, he comprends rien dans la musique,' all said as though he couldn't care less. It was the moment of the Russian Revolution, and we could no longer precede our ballet programmes with the Imperial Anthem. I orchestrated the 'Song of the Volga Boatmen' to replace it, and on the title page of my manuscript Picasso painted a red circle as a symbol of the Revolution.

Picasso drew my portrait at this same time (the first one; the arm-chair portrait was done in his rue de la Boëtie apartment, and the third one was conceived as a mutual gift from Picasso and myself to our friend Eugenia Errazuriz). It was in the Hotel de la Russie, near the Piazza del Popolo, where many of the ballet dancers were staying, including Picasso's future wife Olga (Olga, who had changed his social life; she had many new robes from Chanel to show, besides Picasso, and suddenly the great painter was to be seen at every cocktail party, theatre, and dinner). Picasso was always very generous in making gifts of his art. I have a dozen paintings or drawings given to me by him at various times including some beautiful ink designs of horses drawn on letter envelopes and a fine phallic circle-drawing for a cover of my *Ragtime*.

We journeyed to Naples together (Picasso's portrait of Massine was drawn in the train) and spent some weeks in close company there. We were both much impressed with the

Commedia dell'Arte, which we saw in a crowded little room reeking of garlic. The Pulcinella was a great drunken lout whose every gesture, and probably every word if I had understood, was obscene. The only other incident of our Neapolitan holiday I can remember is that we were both arrested one night for urinating against a wall of the *Galleria*. I asked the policeman to take us across the street to the San Carlo Opera to find someone to vouch for us. The policeman granted our request. Then, as the three of us marched backstage he heard us being addressed as *maestri* and let us go.

Picasso's original *Pulcinella* was very different from the pure Commedia dell'Arte Diaghilev wanted. His first designs were for Offenbach-period costumes with side-whiskered faces instead of masks. When he showed them, Diaghilev was very brusque: 'Oh, this isn't it at all', and proceeded to tell Picasso how to do it. The evening concluded with Diaghilev actually throwing the drawings on the floor, stamping on them, and slamming the door as he left. The next day all of Diaghilev's charm was needed to reconcile the deeply insulted Picasso, but Diaghilev did succeed in getting him to do a Commedia dell'Arte *Pulcinella*. I might add that Diaghilev was equally against my *Pulcinella* music at first. He had expected a strict, mannered orchestration of something very sweet.

4

ABOUT MUSIC TODAY

R.C. What do you mean when you say that critics are incompetent?

I.S. I mean that they are not even equipped to judge one's grammar. They do not see how a musical phrase is constructed, do not know how music is written; they are incompetent in the technique of the contemporary musical language. Critics misinform the public and delay comprehension. Because of critics many valuable things come too late. Also, how often we read criticisms of first performances of new music—in which the critic praises or blames (but usually praises) performance. Performances are of something; they do not exist in the abstract, apart from the music they purport to perform. How can the critic know whether a piece of music he does not know is well or ill performed?

R.C. What does 'genius' mean to you?

I.S. A 'pathetic' term strictly; or, in literature, a propaganda word used by people who do not deserve rational opposition. I detest it literarily and cannot read it in descriptive works without pain. If it doesn't already appear in the *Dictionnaire des idées reçues*, it should be put there with, as its automatic responses, 'Michelangelo' and 'Beethoven'.

R.C. What does 'sincerity' mean to you?

I.S. It is a *sine qua non* that at the same time guarantees nothing.

Most artists are sincere anyway and most art is bad—though of course, some insincere art (sincerely insincere) is quite good. One's belief that one is sincere is not so dangerous, however, as one's conviction that one is right. We all feel we are right; but we felt the same way twenty years ago and to-day we know we weren't always right then.

R.C. Would you 'draw' your recent music? For example:

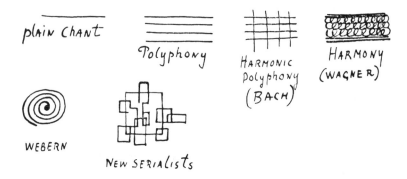

I.S.   This is *my* music:

HARMONY, MELODY, RHYTHM

R.C. You have often remarked that the period of harmonic discovery is over, that harmony is no longer open to exploration and exploitation. Would you explain?

I.S.   Harmony, considered as a doctrine dealing with chords and chord relations, has had a brilliant but short history. This history shows that chords gradually abandoned their direct function of harmonic guidance and began to seduce with the individual splendours of their harmonic effects. Today harmonic novelty is at an end. As a medium of musical construction, harmony offers no further resources in which to inquire and from which to seek profit. The contemporary ear requires a completely different approach to music. It is one of nature's ways that we often feel closer to distant generations than to the generation immediately preceding us. Therefore, the present generation's interests are directed toward music before the 'harmonic age'. Rhythm, rhythmic polyphony, melodic or intervallic construction are the elements of musical building to be explored today. When I say that I still compose 'harmonically' I mean to use the word in a special sense and without reference to chord relations.

R.C. Isn't Busoni's famous 'attempted definition of melody' (1922) a fairly accurate prophecy of the melodic conception of many young composers today? Melody, he said, is 'a series of repeated rising and falling intervals, which are subdivided and given movement by rhythm; containing a latent harmony within itself and giving out a mood-feeling; it can and does exist independently of words as an expression and independently of accompanying parts as a form; in its performance the choice of pitch and of the instrument makes no difference to its essence'.

I.S. The last two points are the most remarkable coming from Busoni. The idea that the actual pitch of the note is not so important in an absolute sense has been supplanted, to my mind, by the idea that pitch matters only because of the interval. Today the composer does not think of notes in isolation but of notes in their intervallic position in the series, in their dynamic, their octave, and their timbre. Apart from the series notes are nothing; but in the series their recurrence, their pitch, their dynamic, their timbre, and their rhythmic relation determine form. The note functions only in the series.

The form is serial, not only some or all of the musical elements that compose it. The individual note determines the form only as part of its group or order.

R.C. Has any new development in the domain of rhythm caught your attention?

I.S. The tempo controls—if tempo comes under the heading of rhythm—in the central movement of *Le marteau sans maître* are an important innovation. In this movement the beat is accelerated or retarded to basic fast or slow metronome speeds with indications *en route* of exactly the speed one should be travelling. This amounts to controlled ritard- and accelerando. Used systematically, as in the *Marteau*, where you are never in a tempo but always going to one, these controls are able to effect a new and wonderfully supple kind of music.

The free-but-co-ordinated cadenzas in Stockhausen's *Zeitmasse* (I have not yet heard his *Gruppen* for three orchestras) are also a rhythmic innovation of great value.

In exploring the possibilities of variable metres young composers have contributed but little. In fact, I have seen no advance on the *Sacre du Printemps*, if I may mention that work, in all the half-century since it was written.

R.C. Do you know that a whole school of *Klangfarbenmelodie* composers is flourishing at present?

I.S. Most of that is the merest stylistic imitation, of course, and nothing could be more ephemeral. But the German word needs definition; it has come to mean too many things. For example, I don't think the *melodie* part of it is good or useful applied to a work such as Webern's *Concerto*, and I am sure that in the same piece *farben* is less important than *klang*-design which isn't the same thing.

If by *Klangfarbenmelodie* you mean no more than a line of music which is divided among two or more instruments, that habit has already reached a *reductio ad absurdum*. Looking at a ridiculously difficult score recently—it was really the map of an idea that had begun not in musical composition but before it—I was reminded of a Russian band I knew in my childhood. This band was made up of twelve open, that is, valveless horns. Each horn had one note to play and together they could produce the chromatic scale. They would practise hours and hours in order to surmount the rhythmic problems presented by simple melodies. I do not see the difference between the idea of this band of hunting horns and the idea of some of the *Klangfarben* scores I have seen.

If a serious composer intends the lines of two or more instruments to produce one melodic line, I advise him to follow Elliott Carter's practice in his string Quartet, and write out the one line reduction as a guide.

ELECTRONIC MUSIC

R.C. Do you have an opinion about *electronic music*?

I.S. I think that the *matière* is limited; more exactly, the composers have demonstrated but a very limited *matière* in all the examples of 'electronic music' I have heard. This is surprising because the possibilities as we know are astronomical. Another criticism I have is that the shortest pieces of 'electronic music' seem endless and within those pieces we feel no time control.

Therefore the amount of repetition, imaginary or real, is excessive.

Electronic composers are making a mistake, in my opinion, when they continue to employ significative noises in the manner of *musique concrète*. In Stockhausen's *Gesang der Jünglinge*, a work manifesting a strong personality and an indigenous feeling for the medium, I like the way the sound descends as though from auras, but the burbling fade-out noises and especially the organ are, I find, incongruous elements. Noises can be music of course, but they ought not to be significative; music itself does not signify anything.

What interests me most in 'electronic music' so far is the notation, the 'score'.

R.C. In the music of Stockhausen and others of his generation the elements of pitch, density, dynamics, duration, frequency (register), rhythm, timbre have been subjected to the serial variation principle. How will the non-serial element of 'surprise' be introduced in the rigid planning of this music?

I.S. The problem that now besets the totalitarian serialist is how to compose 'surprise' since by electronic computer it doesn't exist (though in fact it does, even if every case is computable; even at its worst, we listen to music as music and not as a computing game). Some composers are inclined to turn the problem over to the performer—as Stockhausen does in his *Piano Piece No. XI*. I myself am inclined to leave very little to the performers. I would not give them margin to play only half or selected fragments of my pieces. Also, I think it inconsistent to have controlled everything so minutely and then leave the ultimate shape of the piece to a performer (while pretending that all possible shapes have been allowed for).

R.C. Do you think there is a danger at present of novelty for its own sake?

I.S. Not really. Nevertheless, certain festivals of contemporary music by their very nature cannot help but encourage mere novelty. And, by a curious reversal of tradition, some critics encourage it too. The classic situation in which conservative and academic critics deride the composer's innovations is no more. Now composers can hardly keep up with the demands of some critics to 'make it new'. Novelties sometimes result that could not interest anyone twice. I am more cautious of the power of the acclaimers than of the disclaimers, of those critics who hail on principle what they cannot possibly contact directly with their own ears or understanding. This is

13. With Madame Stravinsky at the opening of an exhibition of
her paintings, New York, January, 1957

(*Columbia Records Photograph*)

14. With Robert Craft (standing) and Pierre Boulez, Hollywood, 1957

musical politics, not music. Critics, like composers, must know what they love. Anything else is pose and propaganda, or what D. H. Lawrence called 'would-be'.

CONTEMPORARY MUSIC AND THE GENERAL PUBLIC

R.C. Isn't the general public everywhere just as isolated from contemporary music since about 1909 as the Soviet Union?

I.S. Not everywhere, not in Germany where, for example, my own later music is performed almost as frequently for the general public as are Strauss and Sibelius in the U.S. But the year 1909 means 'atonality' and 'atonality' did create a hiatus which Marxists attempt to explain as a problem of social pressures when in fact it was an irresistible pull within the art.

R.C. Do you wish to say anything about patronage?

I.S. Haphazard patronage, whether or not it is better than systematic patronage, is extremely inadequate. It called into being all of the music of Schoenberg, Berg, Webern, Bartók, and myself, though most of our music was not called into being at all, but only written and left to compete against more conventional types of music in the commercial market. This is part of the reason why four of those composers died in mid-twentieth century in humiliating circumstances, or at least in circumstances that were far from affluent. This kind of patronage has not changed in a hundred and fifty years except that today there seems to be less of it.

R.C. Do you know the present status of your music east of N.A.T.O.?

I.S. Friends who attended the Warsaw conference of contemporary music in October, 1956, say that my music was officially boycotted there but enthusiastically received nevertheless by composers from the Soviet sphere. My music is unobtainable, all of it and in any form, disc or printed score, east of N.A.T.O.; not only my music but Webern's, Schoenberg's, Berg's, as well. Russia's musical isolation— she will call it our isolation—is at least thirty years old. We hear much about Russian virtuoso violinists, pianists, orchestras. The point is, of what are they virtuosi? Instruments are nothing in themselves; the literature they play creates them. The mandolin and guitar, for instance, did not exist until Schoenberg imagined them in an entirely new way in his *Serenade*. A new musical masterpiece of that kind is a demand that musicians be created to play it. The Soviet virtuoso has no literature beyond the nineteenth century.

I am often asked if I would consent to conduct in the Soviet Union. For purely musical reasons I could not. Their orchestras do not perform the music of the three Viennese and myself, and they would be, I am sure, unable to cope with the simplest problems of rhythmic execution that we introduced to music fifty years ago. The style of my music would also be alien to them. These difficulties are not to be overcome in a few rehearsals; they require a twenty- or thirty-year tradition. I discovered something of the same situation in Germany at the end of the war. After so many years of Hitler in which my *L'Histoire du Soldat*, Schoenberg's *Pierrot lunaire*, Berg's and Webern's music were banned, the musicians were unable for a long time to play the new music, though they have certainly more than made up for it since.

It is the same thing with ballet. A ballet exists in its repertoire as much as, or more than, in the technical perfection of its dancers. The repertoire is a few nineteenth-century ballets. These and sentimental, realist, Technicolor *Kitsch* are all the Soviets do. Ballet in this century means the Diaghilev repertoire and the creations of the very few good choreographers since.

R.C. You have known American musical life since 1925; would

you comment on any aspect of its development since then.

I.S. I hope I am wrong, but I fear that in some ways the American composer is more isolated today than he was in 1925. He has at present a strong tendency to say: 'We'll leave all of that *avant-garde* stuff to Europe and develop our own musical style, an American style.' The result of having already done that is now clear in the way the 'Intellectual advanced stuff' (some of it, that is, for at least ninety-nine per cent of all *avant-garde* products are transparent puerilities) is embarrassing everybody; compared to Webern, for example, most of our simple homespun 'American style' is fatuous in expression and in technique the vilest cliché. In the phrase 'American Music', 'American' not only robs emphasis from 'music' but it asks for lower standards. Of course, good music that has grown up here will be American.

We have no capital for new music as New York was a capital in 1925. Look at the League of Composers' programmes of the nineteen-twenties and see if anything comparable is taking place in New York at the present. Of course, more contemporary music is played there now, and more American music, but the really consequential, controversial, new music is not played, and it was then. True we have those wonderful orchestras, but they are growing flabby on their diet of repertoire and second-rate new music—too much sugar. Recently I was asked to conduct two programmes with one of the glamorous American orchestras. But my programmes were rejected and the engagement cancelled because I refused to play Tchaikovsky instead of a programme entirely of my own music. This could not happen in Europe and at this date it shouldn't happen here. Boards of Directors and managers must stop assuming that their limited educations and tastes are reliable gauges for an audience's. An audience is an abstraction; it has no taste. It must depend on the only person who has (pardon, should have), the conductor.

The United States as a whole have certainly a far richer musical life today, with first-rate orchestras everywhere and good opera production in places like San Francisco, Santa Fé, Chicago, and the universities. But the crux of a vital musical society is new music.

JAZZ

R.C. What is your attitude to jazz?

I.S. Jazz is a different fraternity altogether, a wholly different kind of music making. It has nothing to do with composed music and when it seeks to be influenced by contemporary music it isn't jazz and it isn't good. Improvisation has its own time world, necessarily a loose and large one since only in an imprecisely limited time could real improvisation be worked up to; the stage has to be set, and there must be heat. The percussion and bass (not the piano; that instrument is too hybrid and besides, most of the players have just discovered Debussy) function as a central heating system. They must keep the temperature 'cool', not cool. It is a kind of masturbation that never arrives anywhere (of course) but which supplies the 'artificial' genesis the art requires. The point of interest is instumental virtuosity, instrumental personality, not melody, not harmony, and certainly not rhythm. Rhythm doesn't exist really because no rhythmic proportion or relaxation exists. Instead of rhythm there is 'beat'. The players beat all the time merely to keep up and to know which side of the beat they are on. The ideas are instrumental, or, rather, they aren't ideas because they come after, come from the instruments. Shorty Rogers's[1] trumpet playing is an example of what I mean by instrumental derivation, though his trumpet is really a deep-bored bugle-sounding instrument which reminds me of the keyed bugles I liked so much and wrote for

---

[1] West-coast jazz musician.

116

in the first version of *Les Noces*.[1] His patterns are instrumental: half-valve effects with lip glissandos, intervals and runs that derive from the fingers, 'trills' on one note, for example, G to G on a B-flat instrument (between open and first-and-third fingers), etc.

As an example of what I have said about timing, I can listen to Shorty Rogers's good style with its dotted-note tradition, for stretches of fifteen minutes and more and not feel the time at all, whereas the weight of every 'serious' virtuoso I know depresses me beyond the counter-action of equanil in about five. Has jazz influenced me? Jazz patterns and, especially, jazz instrumental combinations did influence me forty years ago, of course, but not the idea of jazz. As I say, that is another world. I don't follow it but I respect it. It can be an art of very touching dignity as it is in the New Orleans jazz funerals. And, at its rare best, it is certainly the best musical entertainment in the U.S.

THE PERFORMANCE OF MUSIC

R.C. Do you agree that in some cases the composer should indicate how he wishes the conductor to beat his music?

I.S. I think he should always indicate the unit of the beat and whether or not subdivision is to be felt. Also, he should show whether the conductor is to beat the beat or the rhythmic shape of the music if that shape is against the beat. For example, the triplets, three in the time of four, in Webern's *Das Augenlicht* and in my *Surge Aquilo*: I contend that to beat three here (in other words, to beat the music) is to lose the 'in the time of four' feeling, and instead of a triplet feeling you have merely a three-beat bar *in a new tempo*.

R.C. Do you agree with Schoenberg's premise that a good compo-

---

[1] Hearing Mr. Rogers play this instrument in Los Angeles last year perhaps influenced me to use it in *Threni*.

sition is playable in only one tempo? (Schoenberg's example of a piece of music of uncertain tempo was the Austrian hymn from Haydn's *Emperor* Quartet.)

I.S. I think that any musical composition must necessarily possess its unique tempo (pulsation): the variety of tempi comes from performers who often are not very familiar with the composition they perform or feel a personal interest in interpreting it. In the case of Haydn's famous melody, if there is any uncertainty in the tempo the fault is in the alarming behaviour of its numerous interpreters.

R.C. Have you ever considered whether a piece of 'classic' music is more difficult to kill by mis-performance than a 'romantic' piece?

I.S. It depends, of course, on what we decide to mean by those divisions, and also on the kinds and degrees of mis-performance. Let us take refuge in examples, contemporary ones, preferably. My *Agon* and Berg's *Kammerkonzert* divide, I should think, on most of the characteristic issues we imagine to determine those categories.

The *Kammerkonzert* depends strongly on mood or interpretation. Unless mood dominates the whole, the parts do not relate, the form is not achieved, detail is not suffused, and the music fails to say what it has to say—for 'romantic' pieces are presumed to have messages beyond the purely musical messages of their notes. The romantic piece is always in need of a 'perfect' performance. By perfect one means inspired—rather than strict or correct. In fact, considerable fluctuations in tempo are possible in a 'romantic' piece (metronomes are marked *circa* in the Berg, and performance times sometimes diverge as much as ten minutes). There are other freedoms as well, and 'freedom' itself must be conveyed by the performer of a 'romantic' piece.

It is interesting to note that conductors' careers are made for the most part with 'romantic' music. 'Classic' music eliminates the conductor; we do not remember him in it, and we think we need him for his *métier* alone, not for his mediumistic abilities—I am speaking of my music.

But does all of this turned around fit the contrary? Perhaps, though the question of degree is important for the characteristics of each category apply at some point to both. For example, when a conductor has ruined a piece of mine, having failed to convey a sense of 'freedom' and 'mood' let him not tell me that these things are joined exclusively to another kind of music.

R.C. What do you regard as the principal performance problems of your music?

I.S. Tempo is the principal item. A piece of mine can survive almost anything but wrong or uncertain tempo. (To anticipate your next question, yes, a tempo can be metronomically wrong but right in spirit, though obviously the metronomic margin cannot be very great.) And not only my music, of course. What does it matter if the trills, the ornamentation, and the instruments themselves are all correct in the performance of a Bach concerto if the tempo is absurd? I have often said that my music is to be 'read', to be 'executed', but not to be 'interpreted'. I will say it still because I see in it nothing that requires interpretation (I am trying to sound immodest, not modest). But you will protest, stylistic questions in my music are not conclusively indicated by the notation; my style requires interpretation. This is true and it is also why I regard my recordings as indispensable supplements to the printed music. But that isn't the kind of 'interpretation' my critics mean. What they would like to know is whether the bass clarinet repeated notes at the end of the first movement of my *Symphony in Three Movements* might be interpreted as 'laughter'. Let us suppose I agree that it is meant to be 'laughter'; what difference could this make to the performer? Notes are still intangible. They are not symbols but signs.

About Music Today

The stylistic performance problem in my music is one of articulation and rhythmic diction. Nuance depends on these. Articulation is mainly separation, and I can give no better example of what I mean by it than to refer the reader to W. B. Yeats's recording of three of his poems. Yeats pauses at the end of each line, he dwells a precise time on and in between each word—one could as easily notate his verses in musical rhythm as scan them in poetic metres.

For fifty years I have endeavoured to teach musicians to

play   instead of

in certain cases, depending on the style. I have also laboured to teach them to accent syncopated notes and to phrase before them in order to do so. (German orchestras are as unable to do this, so far, as the Japanese are unable to pronounce 'L'.)

In the performance of my music, simple questions like this consume half of my rehearsals: when will musicians learn to abandon the tied-into note, to lift from it, and not to rush the semiquavers afterwards? These are elementary things, but solfeggio is still at an elementary level. And why should solfeggio be taught, when it is taught, as a thing apart from style? Isn't this why Mozart concertos are still played as though they were Tchaikovsky concertos?

The chief performance problem of new music is rhythmic. For example, a piece like Dallapiccola's *Cinque Canti* contains no interval problems of instrumental technique (its Cross shapes in the manner of George Herbert are for the eye and present no aural problems; one does not hear musically-shaped Crosses). The difficulties are entirely rhythmic and the average musician has to learn such a piece bar by bar. He has not got beyond *Le Sacre du Printemps*, if he has got that far. He cannot play simple triplets, much less subdivisions

120

of them. Difficult new music must be studied in schools even if only as exercises in reading.

Myself as a conductor? Well, reviewers have certainly resisted me in that capacity for forty years, in spite of my recordings, in spite of my special qualifications for knowing what the composer wants, and my perhaps one thousand times greater experience conducting my music than anyone else. Last year, *Time* called my San Marco performance of my *Canticum Sacrum* 'Murder in the Cathedral'. Now I don't mind my music going on trial, for if I'm to keep my position as a promising young composer I must accept that; but how could *Time* or anybody know whether I ably conducted a work I alone knew? (In London, shortly after the *Time* episode, I was at tea one day with Mr. Eliot, being tweaked by a story of his, when my wife asked that kindest, wisest and gentlest of men, did he know what he had in common with me. Mr. Eliot examined his nose; he regarded me and then reflected on himself, tall, hunched, and with an American gait; he pondered the possible communalities of our arts. When my wife said 'Murder in the Cathedral', the great poet was so disconcerted he made me feel he would rather not have written this *opus theatricum* than have its title loaned to insult me.)

R.C. Do you agree that perhaps the composer should try to notate 'style' more precisely. For example, in the finale of your *Octuor*, the bassoons play quavers with dots; wouldn't it have been more exact to write semiquavers followed by rests?

I.S. I do not believe that it is possible to convey a complete or lasting conception of style purely by notation. Some elements must always be transmitted by the performer, bless him. In the case of the *Octuor*, for example, if I had written semiquavers, the problem of their length, whether they should be cut off on or before the rests would be substituted for the original problem, and imagine reading all those flags!

R.C. Have you noticed any influence of electronic technique on the compositions by the new serial composers?

I.S. Yes, in several ways; and the electronic technique of certain composers interests me far more in their 'live' compositions than in their electronic ones. To mention only one influence, electronic music has made composers more aware of range problems. But here again, Webern was ahead in realizing that the same material, if it is to be worked out on equal levels, must be limited to four or five octaves (Webern extended beyond that only for important outlines of the form). But electronic music has influenced rhythm (for example, that curious sound which trails off into slower and slower dots), articulation, and many items of texture, dynamics, etc.

R.C. Which of your recorded performances do you prefer, which do you consider definitive?

I.S. I cannot evaluate my records for the reason that I am always too busy with new works to have time to listen to them. However, a composer is not as easily satisfied with recordings of his works as a performer is satisfied for him, in his name, and this is true even when the composer and the performer are the same person. The composer fears that errors will become authentic copy, and that one possible performance, one set of variables will be accepted as the only one. First recordings are standard-setting and we are too quickly accustomed to them. But to the composer-conductor the advantage of being able to anticipate performances of his new works with his own recordings outweighs all complaints. For one thing, the danger of the middle musician is reduced. For another, the time-lag in disseminating new music has been cut from a generation or two to six months or a year. If a work like *Le marteau sans maître* had been written before the present era of recording it would have reached young musicians outside of the principal cities only years later. As it is this same

Marteau, considered so difficult to perform a few years ago, is now within the technique of many players, thanks to their being taught by record.

But the public is still too little aware that the word 'performance' applied to recording is often extremely euphemistic. Instead of 'performing' a piece, the recording artist 'breaks it down'. He records according to the size (cost) of the orchestra. Thus Haydn's *Farewell* Symphony would be recorded from the beginning to the end in order; but *Bolero* would be done backwards, so to speak, if it were sectionally divisible. Another problem is that the orchestra is seated according to the acoustical arrangement required by the engineering. This means that the orchestra does not always sound like an orchestra to the orchestra.

I still prefer productions to reproductions. (No photograph matches the colours of the original nor is any phonographed sound the same as live sound; and we know from experience that in five years new processes and equipment will make us despise what we now accept as good enough imitations.) But the reproduced repertoire is so much greater than the produced, concerts are no longer any competition at all.

MUSIC AND THE CHURCH

R.C. Your *Mass, Canticum Sacrum* and *Threni* are the strongest challenges in two hundred years to the decline of the Church as a musical institution.

I.S. I wish they were effective challenges. I had hoped my *Mass* would be used liturgically, but I have no such aspiration for the *Threni*, which is why I call it not *Tenebrae Service*, but *Lamentations*.

Whether or not the Church was the wisest patron—though I think it was; we commit fewer musical sins in church—it was rich in musical forms. How much poorer we are without the sacred musical services, without the Masses, the Passions, the round-the-calendar cantatas of the Protestants, the motets and Sacred Concerts, and Vespers and so many others. These are not merely defunct forms but parts of the musical spirit in disuse.

The Church knew what the Psalmist knew: music praises God. Music is as well or better able to praise Him than the building of the church and all its decoration; it is the Church's greatest ornament. Glory, glory, glory; the music of Orlando Lassus's motet praises God, and this particular 'glory' does not exist in secular music. And not only glory, though I think of it first because the glory of the Laudate, the joy of the Doxology, are all but extinct, but prayer and penitence and many others cannot be secularized. The spirit disappears with the form. I am not comparing 'emotional range' or 'variety' in sacred and secular music. The music of the nineteenth and twentieth centuries—it is all secular—is 'expressively' and 'emotionally' beyond anything in the music of the earlier centuries: the *Angst* in *Lulu*, for instance (gory, gory, gory), or the tension, the perpetuation of the moment of epitasis, in Schoenberg's music. I say, simply, that without the Church, 'left to our own devices', we are poorer by many musical forms.

When I call the nineteenth century 'secular' I mean by it to distinguish between religious religious music and secular religious music. The latter is inspired by humanity in general, by art, by *Übermensch*, by goodness, and by goodness knows what. Religious music without religion is almost always vulgar. It can also be dull. There is dull church music from Hucbald to Haydn, but not vulgar church music. (Of course there is vulgar church music now, but it is not really of or for the church.) I hope, too, that my sacred music is a protest against the Platonic tradition, which has been the Church's tradition through Plotinus and Erigena, of music as anti-

124

moral. Of course Lucifer had music. Ezekiel refers to his 'tabrets and pipes' and Isaiah to the 'noise of his viols'. But Lucifer took his music with him from Paradise, and even in Hell, as Bosch shows, music is able to represent Paradise and become the 'bride of the cosmos'.

'It has been corrupted by musicians,' is the Church's answer, the Church whose musical history is a series of attacks against polyphony, the true musical expression of Western Christendom, until music retires from it in the eighteenth century or confounds it with the theatre. The corrupting musicians Bosch means are probably Josquin and Ockeghem, the corrupting artifacts the polyphonic marvels of Josquin, Ockeghem, Compère, Brumel.

R.C. Must one be a believer to compose in these forms?

I.S. Certainly, and not merely a believer in 'symbolic figures', but in the Person of the Lord, the Person of the Devil, and the Miracles of the Church.

THE YOUNGER GENERATION

R.C. Of your works, the young *avant-garde* admire *Le Sacre du Printemps*, the *Three Japanese Lyrics*, various of the Russian songs, *Renard*, and the *Symphonies of Wind Instruments*. They react strongly against your so-called neo-classic music, however (*Apollo*, the piano Concerto, *Jeu de Cartes*, etc.), and though they affirm your more recent music they complain that triadic harmonies and tonic cadences are solecisms in the backward direction of the tonal system. What do you say to all this?

I.S. Let me answer the latter complaint first: my recent works *are* composed in the —my— tonal system. These composers are more concerned with direction than with realistic judgments of music. This is as it should be. But in any case they could not have followed the twenty years of their immediate forebears, they had to find new antecedents. A change in direction does not mean that the out-of-influence is worthless however. In science, where each new scientific truth corrects some prior truth, it does sometimes mean that. But in music advance is only in the sense of developing the instrument of the language—we are able to do new things in rhythm, in sound, in structure. We claim greater concentration in certain ways and therefore contend that we have evolved, in this one sense, progressively. But a step in this evolution does not cancel the one before. Mondrian's series of trees can be seen as a study of progress from the more *resemblant* to the more abstract; but no one would be so silly as to call any of the trees more or less beautiful than any other *for the reason that it is more or less abstract*. If my music from *Apollo* and *Oedipus* to the *Rake's Progress* did not continue to explore in the direction that interests the younger generation today, these pieces will none the less continue to exist.

Every age is a historical unity. It may never appear as anything but either/or to its partisan contemporaries, of course, but semblance is gradual, and in time either and or come to be components of the same thing. For instance, 'neo-classic' now begins to apply to all of the between-the-war composers (not that notion of the neo-classic composer as someone who rifles his predecessors and each other and then arranges the theft in a new 'style'). The music of Schoenberg, Berg, and Webern in the twenties was considered extremely iconoclastic at that time but these composers now appear to have used musical form as I did, 'historically'. My use of it was overt, however, and theirs elaborately disguised. (Take, for example, the *Rondo* of Webern's *Trio*; the music is wonderfully interesting but no one hears it as a Rondo.) We all explored and discovered new music in the twenties, of course, but we attached it to the very tradition we were so busily outgrowing a decade before.

About Music Today

R.C. What music delights you most today?

I.S. I play the English virginalists with never-failing delight. I also play Couperin, Bach cantatas too numerous to distinguish, Italian madrigals even more numerous, Schütz *sinfoniae sacrae* pieces, and masses by Josquin, Ockeghem, Obrecht, and others. Haydn quartets and symphonies, Beethoven quartets, sonatas, and especially symphonies like the Second, Fourth, and Eighth, are sometimes wholly fresh and delightful to me. Of the music of this century I am still most attracted by two periods of Webern: the later instrumental works and the songs he wrote after the first twelve opus numbers and before the Trio—music which escaped the danger of the too great preciosity of the earlier pieces, and which is perhaps the richest Webern ever wrote. I do not say that the late cantatas are a decline—quite the contrary—but their sentiment is alien to me and I prefer the instrumental works. People who do not share my feeling for this music will wonder at my attitude. So I explain: Webern is for me the *juste de la musique* and I do not hesitate to shelter myself by the beneficent protection of his not yet canonized art.

R.C. What piece of music has most attracted you from a composer of the younger generation?

I.S. *Le marteau sans maître* by Pierre Boulez. The ordinary musician's trouble in judging composers like Boulez and the young German, Stockhausen, is that he doesn't see their roots. These composers have sprung full-grown. With Webern, for example, we trace his origins back to the musical traditions of the nineteenth and earlier centuries. But the ordinary musician is not aware of Webern. He asks questions like: 'What sort of music would Boulez and Stockhausen write if they were asked to write tonal music?' It will be a considerable time before the value of *Le marteau sans maître* is recognized. Meanwhile I shall not explain my admiration for it but adapt Gertrude Stein's answer when asked why she liked Picasso's paintings: 'I like to look at them'—I like to listen to Boulez.

R.C. What do you actually 'hear' vertically in music such as Boulez's *Deux Improvisations sur Mallarmé* or *Le marteau sans maître*?

I.S. 'Hear' is a very complicated word. In a purely acoustical sense I hear everything played or sounded. In another sense, too, I am aware of everything played. But you mean, really, what tonal relationships am I conscious of, what does my ear analyse, and does it filter the pitches of all the individual notes? Your question implies that you still seek to relate the notes tonally; that you are looking for a 'key' that will enable you to do so (like Hardy's Jude, who imagined that Greek was only a different pronunciation of English). However, all that the ear can be aware of in this sense is density (nobody under thirty, and only rare antediluvians like myself over thirty, uses the word 'harmony' any more, but only 'density'). And density has become a strict serial matter, an element for variation and permutation like any other; according to one's system one gets from two to twelve notes in the vertical aggregation. (Is this mathematical? Of course it is, but the composer composes the mathematics.) All of this goes back to Webern who understood the whole problem of variable densities (a fact so remarkable that I wonder if even Webern knew who Webern was). But the question of harmonic hearing is an older one, of course. Every ordinary listener (if there is any such extraordinary creature) has been troubled by harmonic hearing in the music of the Vienna school from *circa* 1909—in *Erwartung*, for example. He hears all of the notes acoustically but cannot analyse their harmonic structure. The reason is, of course, that this music isn't harmonic in the same way. (In the case of the *Erwartung* recording there is another reason, too; the vocal part is sung off pitch most of the time.)

Do I hear the chord structure of these non-harmonic-bass

15. With the T. S. Eliots at Faber and Faber, London, December, 1958

chords? It is difficult to say exactly what I do hear. For one thing it is a question of practice (while perhaps not entirely a question of practice). But whatever the limits of hearing and awareness are, I shouldn't like to have to define them. We already hear a great deal more in the harmony of these non-tonal-system harmonic pieces. For example, I now hear the whole first movement of Webern's *Symphony* tonally (not just the famous C minor place), and melodically I think everyone hears it more nearly tonally now than twenty years ago. Also, young people born to this music are able to hear more of it than we are.

The Boulez music? Parts of the *Marteau* are not difficult to hear *in toto*; the 'bourreaux de solitude', for instance, which resembles the first movement of the Webern *Symphony*. With a piece like 'après l'artisanat furieux', however, one follows the line of only a single instrument and is content to be 'aware of' the others. Perhaps later the second line and the third will be familiar, but one mustn't try to hear them in the tonal-harmonic sense. What is 'aware of'? Instrumentalists often ask that question: 'If we leave out such and such bits, who will know?' The answer is that one does know. Many people to-day are too ready to condemn a composer for 'not being able to hear what he has written'. In fact, if he is a real composer, he always does hear, at least by calculation, everything he writes. Tallis calculated the forty parts of his *Spem in Alium Nunquam Habui*, he did not hear them; and even in twelve-part polyphony such as Orlando's, vertically we hear only four-part music. I even wonder if in complicated Renaissance polyphony the singers knew where they were in relation to each other—which shows how good their rhythmic training must have been (to maintain such independence).

R.C. How do you understand Anton Webern's remark: 'Don't write music entirely by ear. Your ears will always guide you all right, but you must know why'?

I.S. Webern was not satisfied with the, from one point of view, passive act of hearing: his music requires that the hearer, whether composer or listener, make cognizant relations of what he hears: 'you must know why'. It obliges the *hearer* to become a *listener*, summons him to active relations with music.

THE FUTURE OF MUSIC

R.C. Young composers are exploring dynamics; what kind of new use of them may we expect?

I.S. An example of the kind of dynamic use we might anticipate is in Stockhausen's *Zeitmasse*. In that piece, at bar 187, a chord is sustained in all five instruments, but the intensities of the individual instruments continue to change throughout the duration of the chord: the oboe begins *ppp* and makes a short crescendo to *p* at the end: the flute diminuendos slowly from *p*, then crescendos a little more quickly to *p* where it remains through the last third of the bar; the English horn crescendoes slowly, then more quickly, from *ppp* to *mp*, and diminuendos symmetrically; the clarinet sustains *p*, then slowly diminuendos from it.

Such dynamic exploitation is not new, of course—a serial use of dynamics as well as of articulation, a related subject and just as important, is already clearly indicated in Webern's *Concerto for Nine Instruments*—but I think electronic instruments, and especially electronic control might carry it much farther. I myself employ dynamics for various purposes and in various ways, but always to emphasize and articulate musical ideas: I have never regarded them as exploitable in themselves. In places such as the tenor ricercare in my *Cantata* I ignore volume almost altogether. Perhaps my experience as a performer has persuaded me that circumstances are so different as to require every score to be re-marked for every performance. However, a general scale of dynamic relationships—there are no absolute dynamics—must be clear in the performer's mind.

The inflections of a constantly changing dynamic register are alien to my music. I do not breathe in ritardandos or accelerandos, diminuendos or crescendos, in every phrase. And, infinitely subtle graduations—pianissimi at the limits of audibility and beyond—are suspect to me. My musical structure does not depend on dynamics—though my 'expression' employs them. I stand on this point in contrast to Webern.

R.C. Will you make any prediction about the 'music of the future'?

I.S. There may be add-a-part electronic sonatas, of course, and pre-composed symphonies ('Symphonies for the Imagination' —you buy a tone row complete with slide rules for duration, pitch, timbre, rhythm, and calculus tables to chart what happens in bar 12 or 73 or 200), and certainly all music will be mood-classified (kaleidoscopic montages for contortuplicate personalities, simultaneous concerts binaurally disaligned to soothe both men in the schizophrenic, etc.), but mostly it will very much resemble 'the music of the present'—for the man in the satellite, super Hi-fi Rachmaninov.

R.C. Do you think it likely that the masterpiece of the next decade will be composed in serial technique?

I.S. Nothing is likely about masterpieces, least of all whether there will be any. Nevertheless, a masterpiece is more likely to happen to the composer with the most highly developed language. This language is serial at present and though our contemporary development of it could be tangential to an evolution we do not yet see, for us this doesn't matter. Its resources have enlarged the present language and changed our perspective in it. Developments in language are not easily abandoned, and the composer who fails to take account of them may lose the mainstream. Masterpieces aside, it seems to me the new music will be serial.

ADVICE TO YOUNG COMPOSERS

R.C. Will you offer any cautions to young composers?

I.S. A composer is or isn't; he cannot learn to acquire the gift that makes him one, and whether he has it or not, in either case, he will not need anything I can tell him. The composer will know that he is one if composition creates exact appetites in him, and if in satisfying them he is aware of their exact limits. Similarly, he will know he is not one if he has only a 'desire to compose' or 'wish to express himself in music'. These appetites determine weight and size. They are more than manifestations of personality, are in fact indispensable human measurements. In much new music, however, we do not feel these dimensions, which is why it seems to 'flee music', to touch it and rush away, like the mujik who when asked what he would do if he was made Tsar said: 'I would steal 100 roubles and run as fast as I can.'

I would warn young composers, too, Americans especially, against university teaching. However pleasant and profitable to teach counterpoint at a rich American gynaeceum like Smith or Vassar, I am not sure that that is the right background for a composer. The numerous young people on university faculties who write music and who fail to develop into composers cannot blame their university careers, of course, and there is no pattern for the real composer anyway. The point is, however, that teaching is academic (Webster: 'Literary rather than technical or professional; conforming to rules, conventional; theoretical and not expected to produce a practical result') which means that it may not be the right contrast for a composer's non-composing time. The real composer thinks about his work the whole time; he is not always conscious of this, but he is aware of it later when he suddenly knows what he will do.

R.C. Do you allow that some of the new 'experimental' composers might be going 'too far'?

I.S. 'Experiment' means something in the sciences; it means nothing at all in musical composition. No good musical composition could be merely 'experimental'; it is music or it isn't; it must be heard and judged as any other. A successful 'experiment' in musical composition would be as great a failure as an unsuccessful one, if it were no more than an experiment. But in your question the question that interests me is the one which implies the drawing of lines: 'thus far and no farther; beyond this point music cannot go'. I suppose psychology has studied the effects of various types of challenges on various groups, and I suppose it knows what are normal responses and when they occur—in this case, when one begins to seek defence from new ideas and to rationalize them away. I have no information about this. But, I have all around me the spectacle of composers who, after their generation has had its decade of influence and fashion, seal themselves off from further development and from the next generation (as I say this, exceptions come to mind, Krenek, for instance). Of course, it requires greater effort to learn from one's juniors, and their manners are not invariably good. But when you are seventy-five and your generation has overlapped with four younger ones, it behoves you not to decide in advance 'how far composers can go', but to try to discover whatever new thing it is makes the new generation new.

The very people who have done the breaking through are themselves often the first to try to put a scab on their achievement. What fear tells them to cry halt? What security do they seek, and how can it be secure if it is limited? How can they forget that they once fought against what they have become?

September–December 1957

133

INDEX

(S) stands for Stravinsky

135

Index

Index

137

Index

Index

Index

Wallace, Vice-President, 95

Water Lilies (Monet), 87, 87 n.

Webern, 21, 69, 70, 70 n., 71, 72, 73, 74, 113, 114, 115, 117, 122, 126, 127, 128, 129, 130, 131

Wilder, Thornton, 90

Willaert, 76

With Serov in Greece (Bakst), 97

Wozzeck (Berg), 72

Yeats, W. B., 78, 120

Zborovsky, 87 n.

Zeitmasse (Stockhausen), 110, 130

Ziloti, Alexander, 41 n.

140